SHOOTING TO LIVE

SHOOTING TO LIVE

WITH THE ONE-HAND GUN

BY

CAPTAIN WILLIAM EWART FAIRBAIRN
LATE ASSISTANT COMMISSIONER, SHANGHAI MUNICIPAL POLICE

AND

CAPTAIN ERIC ANTHONY SYKES
LATE OFFICER IN CHARGE SNIPERS UNIT, SHANGHAI
MUNICIPAL POLICE

ILLUSTRATED BY
RANDOLPH SCHWABE, SLADE PROFESSOR OF FINE ART
IN THE UNIVERSITY OF LONDON, MAINLY FROM
PHOTOGRAPHS BY MAJOR F. A. R. LEITAO, SHANGHAI

PALADIN PRESS
BOULDER, COLORADO

Also by W.E. Fairbairn:
All -In Fighting
Defendu
Hands Off!
Get Tough
Scientific Self-Defence

Shooting to Live
by W.E. Fairbairn and E.A. Sykes

Foreword copyright © 2008 by Phil Mathews
Reprint edition 1979, 2008 by Paladin Press
Original edition 1942 by Oliver and Boyd

ISBN 13: 978-1-58160-678-2
Printed in the United States of America

Published by Paladin Press, a division of
Paladin Enterprises, Inc.
Gunbarrel Tech Center
7077 Winchester Circle
Boulder, Colorado 80301 USA, +1.303.443.7250

Direct inquiries and/or orders to the above address.

PALADIN, PALADIN PRESS, and the "horse head" design
are trademarks belonging to Paladin Enterprises and
registered in United States Patent and Trademark Office.

Visit our website at www.paladin-press.com

ERIC ANTHONY SYKES, 1883–1945
THE FORGOTTEN HERO OF COMBATIVES
by Phil Mathews

This passport photograph of E.A. Sykes is courtesy of the estate of the late Col. Rex Applegate.

These photos are from early 1942 while Sykes was with SOE. (Courtesy of James F.)

The life of Eric Anthony (E.A.) Sykes seems to begin and end in mystery. Sykes was one of the true pioneers of what we now term *combatives* (that is, close-quarter combat, whether armed or unarmed), but, as with so many of the instructors of World War II, very little is known about him. All that anyone seems to know is that Sykes was the partner of W.E. Fairbairn in prewar Shanghai, co-designer of the famed Fairbairn-Sykes Fighting Knife, and an instructor to Allied special forces and secret agents during World War II.

As a researcher of the combative arts and their instructors, I know that none of the instructors suddenly appeared out of nowhere to serve the Allies in their time of need. Their service was given freely and was essential to the Allied victory, and many of the trainees who received instruction from the much-needed trainers stated that they owed their very lives to instructions they received from men like Sykes.

With this in mind, whenever I research an instructor I ask myself the following questions: "Who was this man?" "Where did he come from?" "Why have we allowed his memory to be so dishonored that we know so little about him today?"

I cannot let the memory and life's work of Eric Anthony Sykes fade into the obscurity it has met thus far. In my opinion, to not give his legacy the respect and debt of thanks it deserves would be criminal. So I write this.

THE EARLY YEARS

Even the birth of Eric Anthony Sykes has an air of mystery: he was actually born Eric Anthony Schwabe on 5 February 1883 in Barton on Irwill in Lancashire, the eldest son of Lawrence and Octavia Schwabe. Although his own grandfather was of German origin, Sykes' father was a successful British businessman in the cotton trade. His mother was a member of the Ermen family. The Ermens were also cotton merchants and at one time were business partners of the father of Friedrich Engels, coauthor with Karl Marx of *The Communist Manifesto*. Lawrence and Octavia Schwabe were blessed with another son, Randolph, two years after the birth of Eric, and the two brothers were always very close.

Little is known of the schooling of Sykes, but around 1907 it is believed that he made his way abroad to live and work in Shanghai during the so-called "great age" of the British Empire, when colonialism was at its peak. The Schwabes and other elements of the extended family had been conducting business in the Far East (Manila, Hong Kong, Singapore, and Shanghai) since around 1835, but it is not certain whether Sykes had gone there intending to be a part of the family enterprise. In fact, given the family influence in that region, it is somewhat surprising that Sykes chose not to join his family businesses there. Little wonder then that some researchers have inferred that his work in Shanghai was a cover for his service with Britain's Secret Intelligence Services (SIS). On this, all I can say is that the intelligence services of Britain have always maintained closed doors and closed records. I have no materials or contacts in these places to substantiate this allegation.

I was unable to substantiate any service (military or otherwise) that Sykes may have undertaken during the World War I.

THE SHANGHAI YEARS

What is known is that on the 31 May 1917 Sykes changed his surname from Schwabe to Sykes while in Shanghai. At that time, it was popular (and sometimes sensible for self-preservation) for "patriotic Englishmen" across the British Empire with Germanic connections to anglicize their names. In fact, the British royalty, whose family name was Saxe-Coburg, changed the surname to Windsor around that same time. The name changing was mostly because of anti-German sentiment resulting from the costly (and ongoing) war with Germany under Kaiser Wilhelm.

LEGAL NOTICES continued).

Official notice of the name change from Schwabe to Sykes. (Courtesy of David Man.)

At that time, Shanghai still had a British Settlement, and this was where Sykes lived and worked. Sykes is on record as having worked for several companies in Shanghai doing a variety of jobs. Here the history begins to blur again. Sykes ostensibly made his daily living by working in private companies, and it is generally accepted that his friendship with W.E Fairbairn began as a direct result of Sykes being the Shanghai representative for the American companies Colt and Remington. It is believed that Sykes joined the Shanghai Municipal Police Reserve as a special constable in 1926. It was during this time that he and Fairbairn introduced the practice of "bullet marking" on Shanghai Municipal Police (SMP) ammunition.

I know very little of the intervening years until World War II erupted apart from two facts:

- Sykes was still much involved with firearms and training (what would later be termed "defensive tactics" and "use of force on force").
- Sykes married an American divorcée by the name of Catherine Powell, who hailed from Reno, Nevada.

In Sykes' last years in Shanghai, he and Fairbairn worked closely together and became close friends. They collaborated on a book on pistol shooting entitled *Shooting to Live*, which was not published until 1942, long after Fairbairn and Sykes had left Shanghai and were deeply involved in training troops for the war against Germany and Japan. (Paladin Press has published *Shooting to Live* since 1979.)

Shooting to Live is an amazing resource not only on what would later be termed "point shooting" by the firearms community, but also on the reactions of a human being under stress whether shooting or being shot at. At the time Sykes and Fairbairn were there, Shanghai was often described as the "most violent city in the world," and both Sykes and Fairbairn had experienced more than their share of violent encounters in the line of duty. It was these experiences they wrote about in *Shooting to Live*. It was arguably the first of its kind to address that all-too-often forgotten ingredient in any type of personal confrontation—the human element. *Shooting to Live* was also the only publicly published work that I know of to which Sykes ever put his name. As co-author, Sykes was listed as being "Late Officer in Charge Snipers Unit, Shanghai Municipal Police."

Toward the end of the 1930s, most colonials realized that Europe was on a course for war with Germany again. More immediately, the expansion of the Japanese empire into Asia (through Manchuria and then leading south) threatened not only the Southern Chinese states but also Shanghai itself. Bombings and machine gun strafings from Japanese military aircraft into the largely civilian population of Shanghai were daily occurrences. Massive influxes of refugees from outlying areas, coupled with frequent bloody raids by Japanese soldiers, only intensified the existing problems in a city already notorious for its high crime rate. As members of the SMP, Sykes and Fairbairn were on continuous call to deal with one violent event after another, and the official declaration of war in Europe only worsened the situation.

THE EARLY YEARS DURING WORLD WAR II

Both Sykes and Fairbairn retired from the SMP and arrived in Britain in the spring of 1940, little knowing what was in store for them. Soon after their arrival, however, a small and relatively obscure branch of the Secret Intelligence Service known as "Section D" approached Sykes and Fairbairn and soon thereafter both were commissioned as captains by the War Office.

Founded in March 1938, Section D was headed by a colorful major of the Royal Engineers by the name of Lawrence Grand, who, it was rumored, never appeared in public without a "perfectly furled umbrella and a red carnation." Quite surprisingly, Grand was tasked with leading his department to "investigate every possibility of attacking potential enemies by means other than the Operations of Military forces." This meant that Section D's charge was irregular warfare, sabotage, and subversion. In later years, Section D would be remembered as "D for Destruction."

Before the war, Section D had been composed of regular intelligence officers, and through its parent agency, SIS, Section D had missions in most of Europe. But the methods of sabotage and destruction were viewed as an academic exercise by most of its staff. Lectures had been given to various arms of the SIS, but Section D was "caught on the hop" when the war in Europe broke out.

Racing against time, staff from Section D quickly set up hidden arms depots, created "stay-behind" parties in France from former SIS intelligence circuits, and carried out some demolition work, but nothing could halt the Nazi blitzkrieg. At the same time, missions were sent to other countries, such as Poland, but luckily the operatives were able to escape back to England fairly quickly.

Training schools for Section D were established at Brickdonberry and Aston House in Hertfordshire, where Sykes and Fairbairn first started teaching their lessons in close-quarter combat. But not for long.

Where there was once only Section D in the field of irregular warfare, other units quickly sprang up. Created by different people with the same ideas, these units sometimes operated in the same areas, competing for the same manpower and supplies. At one point the Auxiliary Units (stay-behind guerrilla troops created by Colin Gubbins) on the East Coast were trying to do their job while regulars of XII Corps, the local Home Guard, and some of the Admiralty all trained to perform the same role if Germany invaded Britain.

Clearly, something had to be done to clear up the debacle that was threatening to overwhelm the newly created intelligence forces. Soon, lines were drawn in the sand and clear demarcations given at Cabinet level. The Independent Companies (later to become the Commandos) took over raiding functions, Auxiliary Units concerned themselves with stay-behind guerrilla warfare, and Section D merged with the newly created Special Operations Executive (SOE).

So where were Sykes and Fairbairn among all this? As instructors in close combat for Section D, they travelled the length and the breadth of the country, teaching "their brand of mayhem" and training saboteurs, irregulars, stay-behind parties, small- and large-scale raiding forces, and the Home Guard. They also created a small instructor cadre of 12 carefully selected men at Auchinraith House in Scotland to train others in the methods they taught. Bill Pilkington, an original student of both Fairbairn and Sykes, was undisputedly a member of the original 12 students in the first Close Combat Instructor courses.

Brickdonberry, Aston House, Lochailort, and Arisaig were just a few of the many places Sykes and Fairbairn were sent to train students in close combat involving firearms, bladed, blunt, and improvised weapons, as well as unarmed combat. All the above schools began through Section D, even as they separated off to concentrate on their own tasks.

Although Section D was a part of SIS, at the beginning of the war it had no known offices in Shanghai or the rest of the Far East, so it is intriguing to wonder how Sykes and Fairbairn were selected immediately by Section D on their return to Britain, when before the war they were stationed so far away from it all. If not officially a part of SIS, then I believe that one or the other had to be unofficially connected to it.

Col. Rex Applegate believed that Sykes had worked for the SIS while he was in Shanghai, and my research supports the view that it was indeed Sykes and not Fairbairn who had been involved in British intelligence before the war.

THE FALLING OUT BETWEEN SYKES AND FAIRBAIRN

Sadly, the friendship between Fairbairn and Sykes couldn't withstand the strain of war. Both men were fit and active and used to the adrenaline-filled existence of police officers in the world's most dangerous city. Being on the sidelines in time of war would not have suited either of these men of adventure. This thirst for action may have contributed to the rift between the two.

Some researchers cite a reported clandestine attempt by Fairbairn to join a Commando raid that was going into Nazi-occupied territory in late 1941 or early 1942, as one source of the estrangement between Sykes and Fairbairn. As Colonel Applegate related the story, Sykes reported the attempt to authorities as soon as he discovered what Fairbairn was up to, whereupon Fairbairn was removed from the ship before the raid could take place. Reportedly, Fairbairn never forgave Sykes for this. I honestly think the cause of the falling out went deeper than that.

THE SOE YEARS

January 1942 was the real turning point for both Sykes and Fairbairn. Section D's personnel and training schools had been incorporated into SOE, and they found themselves in charge of close-combat training to SOE operatives. But by then the falling out between the two had already occurred, and it had left hard feelings on both sides. Colonel Applegate, who trained with both Sykes and Fairbairn separately, recalled that neither ever spoke of the other. It was fortunate, therefore, that in March 1942—only three months after joining SOE—Fairbairn was sent to STS 103 (Camp X) in Oshawa, Canada, to instruct. Later, Fairbairn went to the American Office of Strategic Services (OSS) and didn't return to the United Kingdom until after the war.

Left to his own devices, Sykes prospered. With Fairbairn's departure, he became the instructor in charge of all SOE's close-combat training. As a part of his duties, he formalized what he termed the "Silent Killing" course, which he and his junior instructors taught to trainees. This became the standard instruction given to all recruit agents in SOE's training schools across the world. The first paragraph in the manual explained that the course was "designed to teach how to fight and kill without firearms. Since the course includes the use of the knife, 'close combat' is not strictly correct. 'Silent Killing' is a more appropriate description."

The first draft of the course syllabus was completed in June 1942. By incorporating intelligence obtained from returning agents, Sykes kept the program updated. The last edition we have available is from December 1943, with an addendum on attacking a sentry inserted in February 1944. The addendum was necessary when it was learned that the Germans had a copy of *Silent Killing* and had changed the way their sentries held their rifles when they patrolled. Fortunately, Sykes modified the instructions to include this change.

In addition to being in charge of SOE's close-combat training, Sykes was tasked with drawing up a program of specialized combat training for what became known as the "Jedburgh Teams." Created in 1943 to help Allied troops liberate occupied Europe, these joint U.S.-British teams were dropped into occupied territory to create as much disturbance as possible, thus denying reinforcements to German troops and tying up much-needed men and arms as Allied troops advanced into German-held territory. Because these teams would create havoc behind the lines until (if ever) they were overrun by their own advancing troops, the chances of a safe return were not high.

When Sykes wrote what became known as "The Jedburgh Manual" in May 1943, he did not know he would be in command of all Jedburgh training at their home base at Milton Hall in Northants.

Perhaps the most well-known description of Sykes' role during this period is from the book *SOE Assignment* by Donald Hamilton-Hall:

> "He taught unarmed combat and quick shooting reactions such as how to kill four people in a room whilst falling down on the ground near the door lintel to make oneself a difficult target. His methods of unarmed combat and silent killing were such that many were able in the years to come to save themselves entirely owing to his instructions."

Sykes was well regarded in SOE. Many of the trainees described him as "looking like a retired bishop," and he acquired the friendly nickname of "Bill" (after the character in Charles Dickens' *Oliver Twist*). Though some have claimed that his nickname was never mentioned to his face, my research indicates that this is misinformation by those who did not know Sykes well.

During his service with SOE, Sykes rose from his original rank of captain with Section D to major in charge of all instruction of unarmed combat, knife, stick, and shooting in SOE at home and abroad. Sykes reached the pinnacle of his career during his SOE service.

THE END

Although an extremely fit man for his age, the strains of training and travel began to take their toll and toward the end of 1944 Sykes began to have serious health problems. While Sykes was in the hospital, SOE doctors reclassified him as "unfit for service." Forced to retire, Sykes left SOE in early 1945 (his official retirement date was 6 April 1945).

Just over a month later, Sykes died on 12 May at a guesthouse in Bexhill on Sea from terminal heart problems, alone and forgotten by the people and agencies he had served so well. He was just 62 years old. His obituary in the *London Times* newspaper was brief:

Sykes did not waste the days after he left SOE brooding about his poor health. For some time before he fell ill, he been writing his own book on self-protection, and it is believed that he spent his last days working on it. Although in the manual Sykes himself stated, "There is nothing new under the Sun," the manual contained his definitive and final thoughts on self-protection, unarmed close combat, and shooting methods. Referred to by researchers today as the "unpublished manual," today it is feared lost.

What is termed World War II combatives today is mostly based on the methodology taught by Sykes so long ago. Although Sykes may be a "forgotten hero of combatives," his legacy lives on today as the techniques he created and taught are being instilled in new generations of fighting men.

morrow (Thursday).

SYKES.—On May 12, 1945, at Bexhill, ERIC ANTHONY (BILL) SYKES (Major, General List, Retired April 6), aged 62. Cremation Charing, Kent, to-morrow (Thursday) at 2.30.

" A Verray Parfit Gentil Knight."

A copy of Sykes' obituary in the London Times. *(Courtesy of James F.)*

• • •

As with all my writings, this is a work in progress. If you have any information about E.A. Sykes that you would like to add or any that you think should be corrected, please contact me at through the publisher.

ACKNOWLEDGMENTS

I would like to thank the following people for their contributions to this work. Without their help, I would not have been able to compile it.

In particular, I have to thank James F. of the United Kingdom (visit his website at www.jimmy-fatwing.com) for allowing me access to his research files. In this field of research, friends are few and far between. Thanks for all your help, mate.

Thanks also go to Stephen Brown for sharing his research files with me. Your generosity is much appreciated.

The following people were also instrumental in my research:

- Paul Gerasimchyk, United States
- Dennis Martin, United Kingdom (visit his website at www.cqbser-vices.com)
- Mika Soderman, Sweden (visit his website at www.get-tough.net)
- Mark Gittins, United Kingdom

A final thanks is owed to the worldwide combatives community. Thank you all and remember to spread the legacy and keep it alive.

REFERENCES

Books

Applegate, Rex, and Chuck Melson. *Close Combat Files of Colonel Rex Applegate*. Boulder, Colo.: Paladin Press, 1998.

Binney, Marcus. *Secret War Heroes: The Men of Special Operations Executive*. London: Holder and Stoughton, UK, 2005.

The Women Who Lived for Danger. New York: William Morrow, 2003 (originally published by Holder and Stoughton, UK, 20-02).

Butler, Rupert. *Hand of Steel: The Enthralling True Story of the Commandos*. London: Hamlyn Publishing, 1980.

Cookridge, E.H. *Inside SOE: The Story of Special Operations in Western Europe 1940–45*. UK: Barker, 1966.

Cunningham, Cyril. *The Beaulieu Finishing School for Secret Agents*. S. Yorkshire, UK: Pen & Sword Books, 1998.

Fleming, Peter. *Operation Sea Lion*. New York: Macmillan, 1975.

Foot, M.R.D. *SOE: The Special Operations Executive*. London: British Broadcasting Corporation, 1984.

Lampe, David. *The Last Ditch: Britain's Resistance Plans against the Nazis*. London: Greenhill Press, 2007.

Mackenzie, William. *The Secret History of Special Operations Executive, 1940–1945*. London: St. Ermin's Press, 2000.

Miller, Russell. *Behind the Lines: The Oral History of Special Operations in World War II*. London: Pimlico, 2003.

Parker, John. *Commandos: The Inside Story of Britain's Most Elite Fighting Force*. UK: Holder-Headline Publishing, 2007.

Spencer-Chapman, F. *The Jungle Is Neutral: A Soldier's Two-Year Escape from the Japanese Army*. Guillford, Conn.: Lyons Press, 2003.

Stafford, David. *Secret Agent: The True Story of the Special Operations Executive*. London: Overlook, 2002.

Turner, Des. *Aston House Station 12: SOE's Secret Centre*. Stroud, Gloucestershire, 2006.

Warwicker, John. *With Britain in Mortal Danger: Britain's Secret Army*. Bristol, UK: Cerberus Publishing, 2002.

West, Nigel. *Secret War: The Story of SOE*. London: Teach Yourself Books, 1993.

Yeaton, Kelly, Samuel S. Yeaton, and Rex Applegate. *The First Commando Knives*. Phillips Publications, 1981, 1996.

Magazine Articles

Thompson, Leroy. "The Shanghai Sniper Rifle." *SWAT Magazine*, September, 1998.

Miscellaneous

Public Records Office, Kew, London.

PREFACE

IT may be said that there is already a sufficiency of books on the one-hand gun and its uses. Some justification for an addition to the list might be considered to exist if the subject could be presented from a different angle, and that is what is now attempted.

Shooting to Live describes methods developed and practised during an eventful quarter of a century and adopted, in spite of their unorthodoxy, by one police organisation after another in the Far East and elsewhere. It is the authors' hope that their relation of these methods may contribute to the efficiency, and therefore safety, of those whose lot it is to use the one-hand gun in the course of duty.

W. E. F.
E. A. S.

1942

CONTENTS

ILLUSTRATIONS

A NOTE FROM THE PUBLISHER

The toughest city in the world was Shanghai. The time was the 1930s. The streets were ruled by gangs. Violent gang wars, murder, rape, and robbery were the order of the day. The night belonged to roaming gangs of toughs. In charge of the Shanghai Municipal Police, Capt. W. E. Fairbairn and his partner, Capt. Eric Anthony Sykes, were determined to reclaim the streets for the citizenry.

Shooting to Live is the product of Fairbairn's and Sykes' *practical* experience with the handgun. Hundreds of incidents provided the basis for the first true book on life-or-death shootouts with the pistol. *Shooting to Live* teaches, in clear, concise terms, all concepts, considerations, and applications of *combat pistolcraft*. The methods taught here provided the basis for all the later masters—Applegate, Weaver, Cooper, Taylor, Chapman, Farnham, Hackathorn, et al. This all-time classic book on combat pistol shooting is a must for the serious shooter.

INTRODUCTION

After the successful retreat of the British Expeditionary force from the shores of Dunkirk in 1940, England began a period of reorganizing its army and strengthening the home guard against the expected German, cross channel invasion. At the same time, training in commando and para military type operations was initiated.

Experts in close quarter fighting techniques, and training, were assembled from all over the commonwealth and allied sources. By the time of Pearl Harbor the most skilled and famous of these men were also engaged in training special intelligence personnel for operations in enemy occupied territory. Schools were operated under tight security conditions all over the English countryside and in Northern Scotland where country estates of the nobility were used as training centers.

In 1942 the U. S. Office of Strategic Services (OSS) under command of Colonel "Wild Bill" Donovan began its program and buildup for similar clandestine operations, with its own personnel, when the main thrust of American military might was ready to aid the allies in retaking occupied Europe. Captain W. E. "Dan" Fairbairn was attached to the OSS for training purposes. The writer, a very willing, "eager beaver" lieutenant, was assigned to him as an assistant for a one year period that was followed by a special duty assignment of the same nature with E. A. "Bill" Sykes in Scotland near the British Commando training center.

By actual records, both Fairbairn and Sykes while with the Shanghai police engaged in over two hundred incidents where violent close combat occurred with oriental criminal elements. These battle scarred veterans were experts in all types of close quarter fighting with and without weapons. Their training techniques and methods were proven first in the back alleys of Shanghai and later with the Commando and the Special Intelligence branches of both the British and U. S. services. *Shooting to Live* was the first written manual to surface in the field of combat pistol shooting. Its principles and techniques were expanded and modified upon to fit American needs in the various editions of the writer's own text, *Kill or Get Killed*. Many present day U. S. military and law enforcement combat handgun shooting techniques can be traced back to this book.

Colonel Rex Applegate

CHAPTER I

PURPOSES OF THE PISTOL

By "Pistol" is meant any one-hand gun. This book is concerned with two types only: (1) pistols with revolving cylinders carrying several cartridges, and (2) self-loading magazine pistols. For convenience, the former will be referred to henceforth as "revolvers" and the latter as "automatics." The word "revolver" has long been accepted by dictionaries in almost every language. If "automatic" has not yet been quite so widely accepted, it is, we think, well on the way to being so, and we shall not be anticipating matters unduly if we continue to use it in the sense indicated.

Excluding duelling (since it is forbidden in most countries and appears to be declining in favour even in those countries in which it is permitted tacitly or otherwise), there seem to remain two primary and quite distinct uses for the pistol. The first of those uses is for target shooting (i.e. *deliberate* shooting with a view to getting all shots in the ten-ring on a stationary target). Its second use is as a weapon of combat.

1

This book is concerned solely with the latter aspect, but it must not be inferred on that account that we in any way decry the sport of target shooting. On the contrary, we admire the high degree of skill for which it calls and which we personally cannot emulate. We recognise the great amount of patient practice necessary to attain such skill, and we can see that in suitable circumstances the inclusion of a target pistol in the camper's equipment would not only be a source of pleasure but might be useful as well. Target shooting has its place and we have no quarrel with it.

There probably will be a quarrel, however, when we go on to say that beyond helping to teach care in the handling of fire-arms, target shooting is of no value whatever in learning the use of the pistol as a weapon of combat. The two things are as different from each other as chalk from cheese, and what has been learned from target shooting is best unlearned if proficiency is desired in the use of the pistol under actual fighting conditions.

These views are the outcome of many years of carefully recorded experience with the Police Force of a semi-Oriental city in which, by reason of local conditions that are unusual and in some respects unique, armed crime flourishes to a degree that we think must be unequalled anywhere else in the world. That experience includes not only armed encounters but the responsibility for instructing large numbers of police in those methods of pistol shooting which

have been thought best calculated to bring results
in the many shooting affrays in which they are called
upon to take part.

There are many who will regard our views as rank
heresy, or worse. We shall be content for the present,
however, if in the light of the preceding paragraph
we may be conceded at least a title to those views,
and we shall hope to fortify the title subsequently
by statistics of actual results of shooting affrays over
a number of years.

At this point it would be advisable to examine very
carefully the conditions under which we may expect
the pistol to be used, regarding it only as a combat
weapon. Personal experience will tend perhaps to
make us regard these conditions primarily from the
policeman's point of view, but a great many of them
must apply equally, we think, to military and other
requirements in circumstances which preclude the
use of a better weapon than the pistol—that is to
say, when it is impracticable to use a shot-gun, rifle
or sub-machine gun.

In the great majority of shooting affrays the
distance at which firing takes place is not more
than four yards. Very frequently it is considerably
less. Often the only warning of what is about to
take place is a suspicious movement of an opponent's
hand. Again, your opponent is quite likely to be
on the move. It may happen, too, that you have been
running in order to overtake him. If you have had
reason to believe that shooting is likely, you will be

keyed-up to the highest pitch and will be grasping your pistol with almost convulsive force. If you have to fire, your instinct will be to do so as quickly as possible, and you will probably do it with a bent arm, possibly even from the level of the hip. The whole affair may take place in a bad light or none at all, and that is precisely the moment when the policeman, at any rate, is most likely to meet trouble, since darkness favours the activities of the criminal. It may be that a bullet whizzes past you and that you will experience the momentary stupefaction which is due to the shock of the explosion at very short range of the shot just fired by your opponent— a very different feeling, we can assure you, from that experienced when you are standing behind or alongside a pistol that is being fired. Finally, you may find that you have to shoot from some awkward position, not necessarily even while on your feet.

There is no exaggeration in this analysis of fighting conditions. Here we have a set of circumstances which in every respect are absolutely different from those encountered in target shooting. Do they not call for absolutely different methods of training ?

To answer this question, we must consider the essential points which emerge from our analysis. They appear to be three in number, and we should set them out in the following order :—

1. Extreme speed, both in drawing and firing.

2. Instinctive, as opposed to deliberate aim.
3. Practice under circumstances which approximate as nearly as possible to actual fighting conditions.

In commenting on the first essential, let us say that the necessity for speed is vital and can never be sufficiently emphasised. The average shooting affray is a matter of split seconds. If you take much longer than a third of a second to fire your first shot, you will not be the one to tell the newspapers about it. It is literally a matter of the quick and the dead. Take your choice.

Instinctive aiming, the second essential, is an entirely logical consequence of the extreme speed to which we attach so much importance. That is so for the simple reason that there is no time for any of the customary aids to accuracy. If reliance on those aids has become habitual, so much the worse for you if you are shooting to live. There is no time, for instance, to put your self into some special stance or to align the sights of the pistol, and any attempt to do so places you at the mercy of a quicker opponent. In any case, the sights would be of little use if the light were bad, and none at all if it were dark, as might easily happen. Would it not be wiser, therefore, to face facts squarely and set to work to find out how best to develop instinctive aiming to the point of getting results under combat conditions ?

It *can* be done and it is not so very difficult.

Everyone is familiar with the fact that he can

point his forefinger accurately at an object at which
he happens to be looking. It is just as easy, moreover, to do so without raising the hand so high as the
level of the eyes. That he can do so may be co-
ordination of eye and hand or just plain instinct,
call it what you will.

Please try this little experiment while sitting at
your desk. Imagine that you are holding a pistol in
your right hand. Sitting squarely and keeping both
eyes open, raise your hand from the level of the
desk, but not so high as the level of your eyes, and
with a straight arm point your extended forefinger
at a mark directly in front of you on the opposite
wall. Observe carefully now what has taken place.
Your forefinger, as intended, will be pointing to the
mark which you are facing squarely, and the back of
your hand will be vertical, as it would be if it
actually held a pistol. You will observe also that
you have brought your arm across you until your
hand is approximately in alignment with the vertical
centre-line of your body and that, under the directing
impulse of the master-eye, your hand will be bent from
the wrist towards the right.

The elements of that little experiment form the
basis of the training system which is elaborated in
succeeding chapters. We cannot claim that the
system produces nail-driving marksmanship, but
that is not what we look for. We want the ability
to hit with extreme speed man-sized targets at very
short ranges under the difficult circumstances which

have been outlined already. Nail-driving marksmanship will not cope with such conditions.

In this training system nothing is permitted to
interfere with the development of speed. For that
reason we have steadily set our faces against competitions or rewards of any kind. The instant that
competitions, with the accompanying medals, badges,
etc., are introduced, men will try to shoot deliberately,
whether consciously or not, and we find our object
is being defeated.

For long shots, and they are necessary occasionally,
different methods must be employed; but even for
long shots speed must still be regarded as essential,
and any tendency to deliberate shooting should be
discouraged by such means as the exposure of the
targets for very brief periods only.

The theories involved in the square stance, the
position of the pistol in line with the vertical centre
of the body, and the hand bent over to the right
have proved in practice to be of immense assistance
in the development of the desired standard of
accuracy when shooting at speed. Though still very
willing to learn, the authors doubt now whether any
other methods would answer the particular purposes
in view. In general, the training system given in this
book may fairly be said to have achieved its object,
but perhaps it is time now for the promised statistics
to play their part in the discussion.

The records of the particular police force of the
semi-Oriental city referred to earlier show that the

force, consistently trained in the methods of this book, has to its credit in twelve and a half years no less than 666 armed encounters with criminals. The following table, referring only to encounters in which *pistols* were used by the police, gives the results :—

	Police.	*Criminals.*
Killed	42	260
Wounded . . .	100	193

CHAPTER II

CHOOSING A PISTOL

WE open this chapter with a warning.

Without an adequate knowledge of its use, there can be few things so purposeless and dangerous as a pistol. Adequate knowledge comes only from competent instruction. If you have never received such instruction and are not prepared to do so, do not buy a pistol, or if you own one already, surrender it to the police. That will help to lighten the burden of their cares.

We shall assume, however, that our readers are sufficiently interested to recognise that the possession of a pistol and efficiency in its use should go hand-in-hand. For them, the starting point in choosing a pistol should be to buy the best they can afford for the particular purpose in view. If a pistol is needed at all it may be needed very badly indeed, and poor quality contributes nothing to either safety or peace of mind.

The type of pistol to be chosen depends on the use to which it is to be put. A pistol that meets the needs of the detective or plain-clothes man, for instance, is not necessarily suitable for individual self-defence or for the uniformed service man.

Let us consider first the case of the detective or plain-clothes man. Here the weapon must be carried concealed and the wearer must be prepared for the quickest of quick draws and an instantaneous first shot, most probably at very close quarters. For that purpose, our own choice would be a cut-down revolver of heavy calibre. Fig. 22 (b) on p. 89 will show you better than any description what we mean.

The weapon shown in the illustration started life as a ·45 Colt New Service double-action revolver with a 5-inch barrel. The hammer spur has been cut off, the barrel length reduced to 2 inches, the front part of the trigger-guard has been removed, and grooves have been cut on the left side of the butt for the middle, third and little fingers.

Now for the reasons for this drastic treatment. The big New Service revolver was chosen, primarily, because the butt is of adequate size for the average man's hand to grasp in a hurry without any fumbling. Secondly, it is one of the most powerful weapons possible to obtain.

The removal of the hammer spur and the smoothing over of what remains prevent the weapon from catching in the clothing when drawn in a violent hurry. As the hammer cannot be cocked by the thumb, the weapon has to be fired by a continuous pull on the trigger. With a sufficiency of practice, very fast shooting is rendered possible by this method.

The shortening of the barrel is for speed in drawing.

Obviously, it takes less time for 2 inches of barrel to emerge from the holster than 5 inches. Contrary to what might be expected, there is no loss of accuracy, at any rate at the ranges at which the weapon is customarily used.

The front part of the trigger-guard is removed in order to eliminate yet another possible cause of fumbling when speed is the order of the day. The index-finger, no matter of what length or thickness, wraps itself in the proper position round the trigger without any impediment whatever. The grooves on the butt are there to ensure that the fingers grip the weapon in exactly the same way every time.

Lest it be thought that we are the originators of this fearsome but eminently practical weapon, let us say at once that we are not. We owe the idea to a book by Mr J. H. Fitzgerald of the Colt's Patent Fire Arms Manufacturing Company, and we gladly acknowledge our indebtedness.

For a weapon to be carried openly by uniformed police and officers and men of the fighting services, we unhesitatingly avow our preference for the automatic pistol. We shall treat it as a matter of personal preference and shall not abuse the supporters of the revolver for having other views. They are quite welcome to those views and we trust we may be allowed to retain ours. We shall do so, in any case, until we have good reason to alter them.

We are familiar with the criticisms so often made

of the automatic pistol. It is said that it is un-
reliable, will often jamb without provocation and
certainly will do so if mud, sand or water gets into
the mechanism, and above all, it is not safe.

There have been and possibly still are automatics
like that, but one is not obliged to use them.

We think it is only in Great Britain that the
reliability of the automatic is still questioned. In
the United States, while many people adhere to
their preference for the revolver, we have never
heard any doubts expressed in the matter, and it is
worthy of note that both there and in Germany the
automatic has long been in use as a standard weapon
of the fighting services.

There are in existence types of automatic pistols
which are perfectly reliable. We base this statement
on our actual experience of them over a period of
twenty years. That experience includes an intimate
knowledge of a service consisting of over six thousand
men, most of them armed with automatics and having
a surprising record of shooting affrays to their credit.
If their weapons had been in any way unsatisfactory,
twenty years should have sufficed to reveal the
defects. But in all that time nothing has occurred,
either in the training of the service referred to or
in the affrays in which the service has taken part,
to cast the slightest doubt on the reliability of the
automatic, nor has there been a single instance of
injury or death due to accident.

Apart from the question of reliability, we have

found that in comparison with the revolver, the automatic offers the following advantages :—

It is easier and quicker to recharge.
It can be fired at far greater speed.
It is easier to shoot with.

The first point will be readily conceded but the other two may meet with opposition.

It is probably the case that, *for the first shot*, the cut-down revolver which has been described is fractionally quicker, but for subsequent shots the rate of fire of the automatic is much higher. A great deal of the recoil is absorbed in the operation of the mechanism and the trigger pull is much shorter and easier than that of the revolver. We refer, of course, to the use of the double-action revolver. If the hammer were to be cocked for each shot, the rate of fire would be funereal by comparison. A skilled shot can do excellent work with the automatic even while making it sound like a machine-gun.

It seems to follow logically that the absorption of so much of the recoil, combined with the shorter trigger-pull, furnish theoretical proof of our contention that the automatic is easier to shoot with. Practical proof of our contention is found in the training results. Critical observation has demonstrated that a beginner can be trained in the use of the automatic in a third of the time and with the expenditure of less than half the ammunition required for the revolver. Furthermore, once trained in the use of the automatic, men appear definitely to need less subsequent practice to maintain the standard of shooting which has been attained in the course of training.

We shall endeavour to throw more light on this subject in the chapters on training methods, and by way of preface to those chapters we must introduce and describe one more point in connection with the automatic, and this time we shall certainly be accused of heresy.

We have an inveterate dislike of the profusion of safety devices with which all automatic pistols are regularly equipped. We believe them to be the cause of more accidents than anything else. There are too many instances on record of men being shot by accident either because the safety-catch was in the firing position when it ought not to have been or because it was in the safe position when that was the last thing to be desired. It is better, we think, to make the pistol permanently " unsafe " and then to devise such methods of handling it that there will be no accidents. One of the essentials of the instruction courses which follow is that the pistols used shall have their side safety-catches permanently pinned down in the firing or " unsafe " position. How this matter is taken care of is described at length in Chapter III. Suffice it to say here that our unorthodox methods have been subjected to the acid test of many years of particularly exacting conditions and have not been found wanting.

Having dealt with weapons suited to the detective or plain-clothes man and the uniformed services respectively, there remains the case of the private individual who wishes to carry a gun. In most countries it is illegal to do so and we have no wish to encourage law-breaking. Nevertheless, there are still some countries and circumstances in which it may be necessary and advisable for the private individual to go armed.

Our recommendation to the private individual who can justifiably claim the right to carry a pistol is to buy an automatic and carry it in a shoulder holster such as is described in a succeeding chapter. We are not greatly in favour of small weapons. No small weapon can possess the strength and reliability of a large one. The material and work-manship may be as good but the margins of tolerance are too small to provide the absolute reliability which is so desirable. We recommend the automatic of good size and calibre partly because we are assured of its reliability and partly because of its shape. It does not " bulge " like the revolver and therefore is less noticeable (we are presuming that the private individual will carry his pistol concealed). Do not forget the obligation which you are under to make yourself thoroughly safe and efficient with the weapon of your choice.

We are often asked what is the best weapon to

have in the house for purely protective purposes. Most of the people who make this enquiry know little of fire-arms and say so quite frankly. It usually happens, too, that they have neither the intention nor the opportunity to make themselves efficient with any kind of one-hand gun. If they are of this type, we are convinced that they would be better off with a good watch-dog, or even a police-whistle. There are, however, many men whose knowledge of fire-arms is limited to the shot-gun, in the use of which they are both proficient and reliable. If this type of man insists on possessing some kind of weapon " to keep in the house " we would recommend him to acquire a " sawn-off " shot gun, with external hammers of the re-bounding type and barrels of about 18 inches in length. The ease with which it can be manipulated, the accuracy with which it can be aimed, either from the shoulder or the hip, and the spread of the shot charge combine to make it a much safer and more efficient weapon than any kind of one-hand gun in the use of which he is not proficient.

CHAPTER III

TRAINING : PRELIMINARY COURSE FOR RECRUITS

THE course of instruction which follows relates primarily to the Colt automatic. The elimination by us of any use of the side safety catch necessitates the introduction of special features, and the system consequently differs considerably from that in use by the American forces, who are armed with this particular weapon.

It might be thought that it would have been better to have devised separate courses of instruction for revolver and automatic respectively, but in actual fact that would have entailed going over the same ground twice. The methods of instruction given in this chapter apply equally to any pistol, revolver or automatic, if the reader will regard them from two aspects, making a careful distinction between the two. The first of those aspects is merely that of the mechanics of the Colt automatic and, with suitable modifications due to differences of design, applies equally to any other automatic. The second relates solely to *the method of shooting* and that, without any modification whatever, applies equally to any form of one-hand gun from the flint-lock onwards. The revolver user who wishes to make use of this

chapter has only to disregard, therefore, anything
which obviously relates to the mechanics of the Colt
automatic. He will have uo difficulty in doing
that.

The mechanics of the revolver are so simple and
so familiar by now to everyone that it is unnecessary,
we think, to include any description of them. We
would emphasise, however, our preferences for the
very firm grip, with the fully extended thumb, the
exclusive use of the double-action, firing in bursts,
for all short range shooting and for the single-action
at longer ranges, in circumstances which afford the
necessary time for its use. Speed with the double-
action is attainable more easily than is generally
thought, but only by training the trigger-finger by
means of continual snapping practice.

The instructor should commence by taking up a
pistol and " proving " it. This is done by removing
the magazine, working the slide back and forth
several times, and finally pulling the trigger. The
insertion of a magazine and the loading and unloading of the pistol should then be demonstrated
and explained. Each operation is described in detail
and illustrated in the following pages. This is the
moment for the instructor to point out and give the
reason for the pinning-down, out of action, of the
safety-catch on the left-hand side of the pistol. He
should make it perfectly clear that the pistol, when
carried on service, should have a charged magazine
inserted but that *it should never be carried with a*

round in the breech. He should show that when it is desired to fire all that has to be done is to load in the manner described in para. 2 (*c*). He should then proceed to demonstrate the extreme speed with which it is possible to draw, load and fire by this method, which compares more than favourably with the alternative of drawing, pulling down the safety-catch and firing a round already in· the breech. It should be shown, too, that the first method (with the breech empty) eliminates the fumbling and un-certainty inherent in the use of the safety-catch.

With this preface, all is now ready for the course to commence.

1. ONE HOUR'S " DRY " PRACTICE

(*a*) On taking the pistol in the hand, we recommend, as an aid to accurate pointing, that the thumb be fully extended and pointing forward in the same plane as the pistol barrel (Fig. 1).

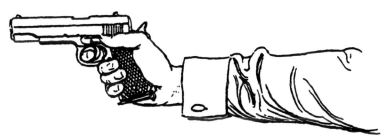

FIG. 1.—The Correct Grip.

(*b*) Stand square with the target, gripping the pistol now as if it weighed twenty or thirty pounds, pistol arm straight, rigid and across the body (Fig. 2). Bend the hand slightly to the right, to bring the pistol exactly in line with the vertical centre-line of the body (Fig. 3).

(c) Raise the pistol (pistol arm still rigidly straight and pivoting from the shoulder), keeping it exactly· in line with the vertical centre-line of the body until it covers the aiming mark on the target (Fig. 4). Both eyes are to be kept open and the recruit simply sees the target surrounding his pistol, making no attempt to look at or line up the sights, or to let the master-eye control the aim.

(d) Immediately the aiming mark is covered, pull the trigger and lower the pistol to the position shown in Fig. 3 (the " ready " position).

Notes

Paragraphs (b) and (c) in conjunction with Fig. 4 reveal a deliberate attempt to eliminate *conscious* control by the master-eye. Instead, the aim is controlled by the combination of the square stance and the manner of holding the pistol, *i.e.* in the centre of the body, with the hand bent over to the right, elements which were employed unconsciously in the experiment on page 6. The mastery of this combination is all that is required for effective aiming at short range, a point which will emerge more clearly,

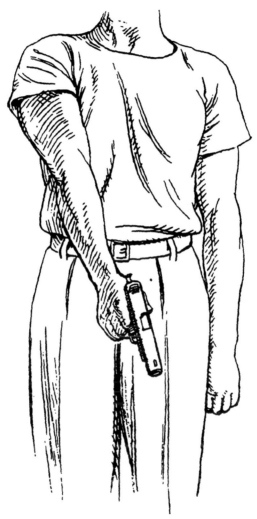

Fɪɢ. 2.—Preliminary to Ready Position.

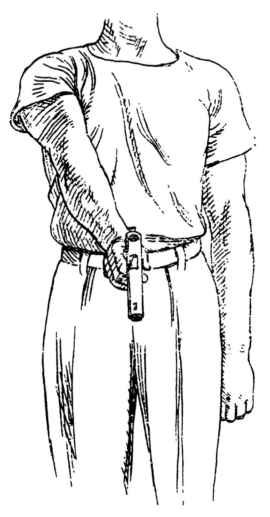

FIG. 3.—Ready Position.

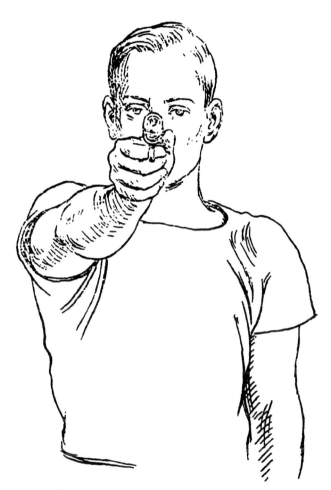

FIG. 4.—Firing, Arm Fully Extended.

perhaps, in the next chapter in discussing shooting with the pistol held well below the line of sight.

Trembling due to the firm grip will *not* cause a wild shot.

The trigger must be released, not by violent pressure of the forefinger alone but by increasing pressure of the whole hand. The combination of the very firm grip and the pressure of the fully-extended thumb are of great assistance in the proper release of the trigger.

The firm grip helps also in two other ways. It ensures smoother action in raising the pistol from the " ready " (Fig. 3) to the firing position (Fig. 4) and it counteracts the tendency to raise the pistol higher than the point of aim.

2. One Hour's Practice in Safety Precautions Loading and Unloading

(a) Demonstrate the proper ways of charging and uncharging magazines. To charge, press cartridges downwards against the forward end of either the magazine platform or the topmost cartridge, as the case may be, sliding the cartridge rearwards *under* the inwardly curving lips of the magazine. If cartridges are forced vertically downwards past these lips, the magazine cannot escape deformation. To uncharge, hold the magazine in the right hand and eject the cartridges one by one by pressure of the right thumb on their bases. The cartridges should be caught in the left hand and on no account should they be allowed to drop on the ground.

(b) Hold the pistol as in Fig. 5. Insert the charged magazine. To make sure that it is locked in place, push up, with the left thumb, on the base plate of the magazine. Relax the pressure, and it will be obvious by touch whether the magazine is locked.

(c) *To load the pistol* turn it over, as in Fig. 6, grasping the slide firmly with the thumb and forefinger of the left hand. Push forward with the right hand until the slide is felt to be open to its fullest extent (Fig. 7). Immediately that point is reached, release the hold with the left hand. The slide flies forward, taking with it and forcing into the breech the topmost cartridge of the magazine, the pistol pointing to the ground meanwhile (Fig. 8). Turn the hand to the " ready " position (Fig. 3), the pistol being now cocked and ready for action.

(d) *To remove the magazine,* hold the pistol as in Fig. 9 and release the magazine by pressing the magazine catch with the left thumb. The magazine must be caught in the palm of the left hand and should then be restored to pouch or pocket, as the case may be, or handed to the instructor if the latter so directs. The pistol meanwhile *must* be kept pointing to the ground, since it is still cocked

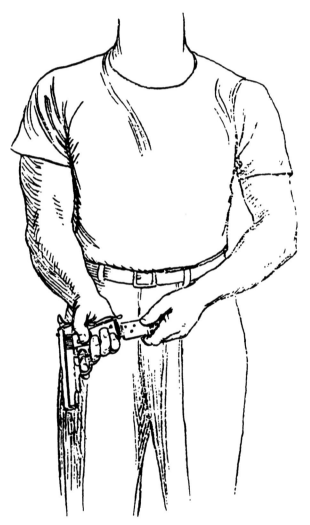

FIG. 5.—Inserting Magazine.

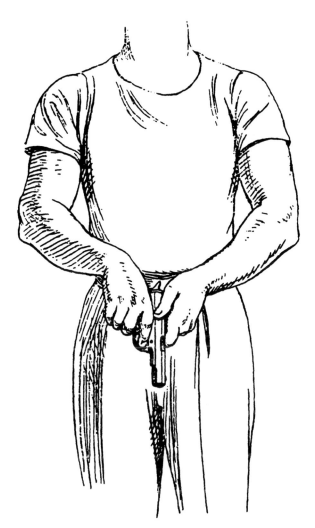

FIG. 6.—First Position of Loading.

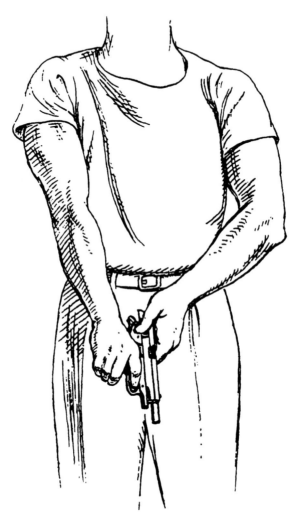

FIG. 7.—Second Position of Loading.

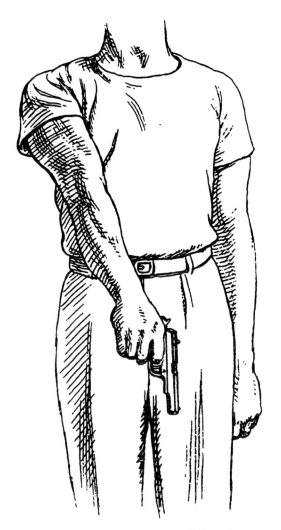

FIG. 8.—Third Position of Loading.

FIG. 9.—Removing Magazine.

and has a live round in the breech. The magazine being disposed of, turn the pistol with the wrist into the position of Fig. 10, and eject the live round by pulling back the slide with the finger and thumb of the left hand (with a little practice the live round can be saved from damage by catching it in the left hand as it is ejected). Work the slide back and forth a few times, as an added measure of safety, and pull the trigger, the pistol pointing all the while to the ground.

(e) *Dismounting the pistol for cleaning.* A knowledge of how to dismount the pistol, as far as is necessary for cleaning and of assembling it subsequently, is essential, and this is a convenient stage in the proceedings at which to teach it. It provides also a good opportunity to impress on the recruit the necessity for *always* treating a pistol as loaded until proved otherwise. Before he is allowed to place his pistol on the bench on which it is to be dismounted, the weapon is to be " proved " by removing the magazine, working the slide back and forth several times and pulling the trigger, the pistol being held as shown in Figs. 9 and 10.

Note

" Dummy " ammunition should be used throughout this practice.

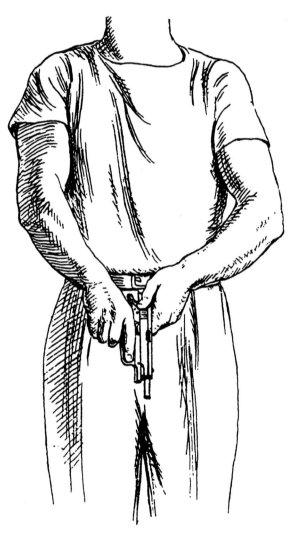

FIG. 10.—Working the Slide.

3. INITIAL FIRING PRACTICE

(a) The target should be white, not less than 8 feet square and should have in the middle a life-size outline of a man, full view (Fig. 11). The recruit is to stand not more than 2 yards away from this target. The size of the target and the distance at which the recruit is to fire need explanation. The combination of these two factors renders it almost impossible for even the most awkward beginner to score a clean miss. With every shot registered, the instructor sees plainly what fault has been committed and is at once able to correct it. The recruit experiences pleasurable surprise that even he is able to hit the target, and that is a much better beginning to his training than the mortification of missing a small target altogether, without knowing in the least where his shot has gone. In short, by the use of these methods the instructor has far less trouble, the recruit gains confidence, and whoever has to pay for it is saved a whole lot of ammunition.

(b) Target and distance as above, the recruit is given six cartridges. After charging his magazine, inserting it in the pistol and putting one round in the breech, all as described in para. 2 (sections (a), (b) and (c)), the recruit stands at the " ready " position.

C

He should then be told to keep both eyes open, concentrate his gaze on the centre of the figure

FIG. 11.—Recruits' Target.

target, bring the pistol up quickly and, as described in para. 1 (sections (c) and (d)), fire immediately it covers that point on the target on which his eyes are focussed, returning subsequently to the " ready " position without delay. Repeat until the recruit has fired four out of his six shots. The last two shots should be fired as a " burst," *i.e.* in succession and as rapidly as the recruit can manage. He should remain afterwards in the firing position until told by the instructor to lower his arm to the " ready."

Notes

This practice should not be hurried. The first four shots, as each is fired, should be pointed out on the target, the recruit standing at the " ready " while the instructor explains the causes of any which are badly placed. The causes are normally simple enough—hand insufficiently bent to the right, " dipping " the hand downwards, or not gripping firmly enough to prevent the trigger from being " yanked off." If the two rapid-fire shots are widely apart it is conclusive evidence of a loose grip.

The instructor should not be content u les` his explanations produce an immediate improvement in the recruit's shooting. These recruits who are not firing should be " fallen in " eight to ten yards in rear of the firing point. From there they can watch the shooting and its results. They should be permitted to talk but not loudly enough to prevent the man who is shooting from hearing what the instructor is saying.

4. SECOND FIRING PRACTICE

(a) Same target and distance.

(b) Hand the recruit a magazine containing one "dummy" and five live rounds. The "dummy" is to be included without the recruit's knowledge and its position in the magazine should be different for each man who takes his turn at the firing point. Men waiting to fire should not be allowed to watch the practice described below.

(c) The recruit is to fire as previously but this time in three "bursts" of two shots each. Errors of aiming should be corrected between "bursts."

(d) When the "dummy" round is arrived at, treat it as a misfire. Have the recruit eject it *immediately* and carry on firing his next burst *without any delay*.

(e) At the conclusion of this practice, explain to the recruit that it is useless, wasteful of time and extremely dangerous to look down the muzzle of his pistol when he has a misfire. Some of them *will* do it. Explain also that a bad jamb can be caused by covering the ejector cut with the left hand when retracting the slide in order to eject a cartridge. This is a fault which is frequently found and should be corrected as soon as possible in the training course. See Fig. 10, p. 32, for how it ought to be done.

5. THIRD FIRING PRACTICE

Repetition of practice given under para. 4 but this time at 4 yards. If the recruit's shooting has been satisfactory so far, he may be allowed to fire this practice in two " bursts " of three rounds each.

Notes

The instructor will be well advised to give his pupils short " rest " periods at fairly frequent intervals and to utilise such intervals to impress upon them the conditions under which they may be called upon to use their pistols eventually. Reference to Chapter I (pp. 3-4) will indicate the general line to take, the points requiring special emphasis being the short range at which most encounters take place, the likelihood of unfavourable light and terrain, the advisability of firing in " bursts " and the paramount importance of speed. If prominence is given to points of that nature, recruits will be assisted to comprehend more readily the reasons underlying the instruction they are receiving. It will be plain to them, for instance, that they must not look at their sights because they will never have time to do so, that they must grip their pistols hard because that is what they will do infallibly in the stress of actual combat, and that, when obliged to shoot, they will have to do so with all the aggressiveness of which they are capable.

CHAPTER IV

TRAINING : ADVANCED METHODS

CHAPTER III has taken care of all the stages of the recruit's preliminary training, but before he is turned loose on the world as qualified to use a pistol there is one more thing for him to learn. This is shooting from what, for want of a better term, we call the " three-quarter hip " position illustrated in Fig. 12.

This position is designed to meet a condition referred to in the first chapter when describing the circumstances under which shooting affrays are likely to take place. We indicate there that in moments of stress and haste men are apt to fire with a bent arm.

Examination of the illustration shows exactly this position. Closer examination shows also that the firer is facing his adversary squarely, has one foot forward (it does not matter which), and that he is crouching slightly.

From this position, pistol hand in the vertical centre-line of the body and hand bent to the right as before, the recruit fires a burst of two or three shots, but *quickly*, at a distance of 3 yards. If he succeeds in making nothing worse than a 6-inch group, he should repeat the practice at 4 yards.

The instructor should make a special point of

explaining all the elements of this practice. The bent arm position is used because that would be instinctive at close quarters in a hurry. The square stance, with one foot forward, is precisely the attitude in which the recruit is most likely to be if he had to fire

FIG. 12.—" Three-quarter Hip " Position.

suddenly while he was on the move. The " crouch," besides being instinctive when expecting to be fired at, merits a little further explanation.

Its introduction into this training system originates from an incident which took place in 1927. A raiding party of fifteen men, operating before daybreak, had to force an entrance to a house occupied by a gang of criminals. The only approach to the house was through a particularly narrow alley, and it was expected momentarily that the criminals would open fire. On returning down the alley in daylight after the raid was over, the men encountered, much to their surprise, a series of stout wires stretched at intervals across the alley at about face height. The entire party had to duck to get under the wires, but no one had any recollection of either stooping under or running into them when approaching the house in the darkness. Enquiries were made at once, only to reveal that the wires had been there over a week and that they were used for the wholly innocent purpose of hanging up newly dyed skeins of wool to dry. The enquiries did not, therefore, confirm the suspicions that had been aroused, but they did serve to demonstrate conclusively and usefully that every single man of the raiding party, when momentarily expecting to be fired at, must have crouched considerably in the first swift traverse of the alley. Since that time, men trained in the methods of this book have not only been permitted to crouch but have been encouraged to do so.

The qualification we require before the recruit's course can be successfully passed is 50 per cent of hits anywhere on the man-sized targets employed. Time has shown this to be adequate for the purpose in view.

We indicate elsewhere our aversion to trophies,

badges, etc. No "expert's" or "marksman's" badges are issued to men who pass our recruit or other courses, no matter how much in excess of 50 per cent. their scores may have been. If a man makes "possibles" throughout, his only reward is the resultant confidence in himself and the satisfaction of knowing that if he has to "shoot it out" with a pistol he will be a better man than his opponent.

Similarly, we have a dislike of "team shoots." We feel that the ammunition would be much more usefully employed in giving additional practice under instruction.

From now on, in proceeding to more advanced training, the use of stationary targets should be abandoned in favour of surprise targets of all kinds and in frequently varied positions. Such targets would include charging, retreating, bobbing, and traversing figures of man-size. Traversing targets can be either at right or oblique angles. Musketry officers will have no difficulty in devising for themselves endless variations on this theme, and current incidents, more especially in the nature of actual happenings to men of their particular service, often provide valuable suggestions.

We will give one example of a practice which has been frequently carried out with good results. It is designed not only as a test of skill with the pistol under difficult conditions, but also a test of bodily fitness and agility, qualities which to the policeman at any rate are every bit as necessary in the circumstances which are so often encountered in shooting affrays.

In this practice, which we have called the " Pursuit," the shooter is started off at the run, outside the range, on an obstacle course consisting of jumping a ditch, running across a plank over water, crawling through a suspended barrel, climbing a rope, a ladder, and over a wall, finishing up with a 100 yards dash ending at 4 yards from the targets. Without warning or waiting, two surprise targets are pulled, one after the other, and at each he fires a " burst " of three shots. The targets are exposed for no longer than it takes to fire three shots at the highest possible speed.

Yet another practice, a " mystery shoot," is described in the chapter entitled " A Practical Pistol Range."

In all practices at surprise targets, opportunity must be found for the performance of two very essential operations. In order of importance, these are :—

1. Making safe after firing only a portion of the contents of the magazine.
2. Inserting a second magazine after totally expending the contents of the first and continuing to fire without delay.

In the first instance, after firing one or two shots from a fully charged magazine, the instructor should give the order to cease fire. The shooter should then come to the "ready," remove the magazine, eject the live round from the breech, work the slide back and forth several times and finally pull the trigger, all as described on pp. 25 and 31 (Figs. 9 and 10).

In the second instance, immediately the last shot has been fired, the shooter comes to the "ready," removes the empty magazine, inserts a fresh one and reloads, either by pressing down the slide release stop with the thumb of the left hand or by slightly retracting and then releasing the slide. The slide flies forward, taking a cartridge into the breech, and the shooter resumes the "ready" position by bending his hand to the right and awaits the appearance of the next target.

Practice at surprise targets can be carried out first with the arm fully extended and later from the "three-quarter" hip position. There are still two other methods of close-quarter shooting to be described, but before doing so this will be perhaps an opportune moment to call the attention of instructors to several points which will be of assistance in getting results.

When firing at surprise targets, never let men anticipate matters by standing in the firing position. They must be standing at the "ready" before the first target appears. If the succeeding targets are pulled with no perceptible interval, the men may continue to stand in the firing position. Otherwise they should come down to the "ready" again after each shot or " burst " while awaiting the appearance of the next target.

Attention has been drawn already to the necessity for the square stance. When turning from one target to another the square stance must be preserved by turning the body. This can be effected by scraping the feet round or even jumping round if the extent of the turn warrants it. It does not matter how it is done so long as the firer faces each fresh target squarely and is thus enabled to retain the pistol in its original position, *i.e.* in alignment with the vertical centre-line of the body.

In firing at a crossing target (" running man "), it will soon be observed that 90 per cent. of all the misses are traceable to firing ahead of it or, as a man accustomed to the shot-gun would say, to " leading it." This holds good even when the range is only 4 yards and the target only travels at about 3 miles an hour. This is not the place for a controversy over the rival merits of " leading " a moving target or " swinging " with it. Our purpose is merely to assist instructors in correcting their pupils' mistakes, and we content ourselves with pointing out that, distance and speed of target being as stated, a bullet travelling at eight hundred feet a second would strike only about three-quarters of an inch behind the point of aim.

We now turn to the two other methods of close-quarters shooting previously referred to. These are, respectively :—

The " half-hip " (Fig. 13).
The " quarter " or " close-hip " (Fig. 14).

Apart from shortening the arm by bringing the elbow
to the side, the " half-hip " is no different from the
" three-quarter," and should be practised at not
more than 3 yards. Above that distance it would
be more natural to shoot from the " three-quarter "
position.

The " quarter " or " close-hip " position is for
purely defensive purposes and would be used only
when the requirements are a very quick draw, followed
by an equally quick shot at extremely close quarters,
such as would be the case if a dangerous adversary
were threatening to strike or grapple with you.
Practise this at 1 yard. This is the only position in
which the hand is not in the centre of the body.

Before we close the subject of shooting at short
ranges, we would ask the reader to keep in mind that
if he gets his shot off first, no matter whether it is a
hit or a miss by a narrow margin, he will have an
advantage of sometimes as much as two seconds
over his opponent. The opponent will want time to
recover his wits, and his shooting will not be as
accurate as it might be.

It will be appropriate now to turn our attention
to training ourselves for shooting at longer ranges,
for in spite of having said that the great majority
of shooting affrays take place within a distance of
4 yards, the need does arise occasionally for a
long shot.

FIG. 13.—" Half-Hip " Position.

FIG. 14.—" Quarter " or " Close-Hip " Position.

For a long shot in the standing position, we think the two-handed methods shown in Figs. 15 and 15A

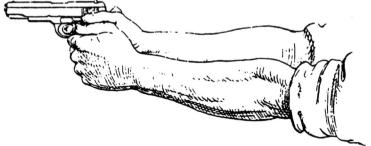

FIG. 15.—Two-Handed, Standing.

are best calculated to produce results. The right arm is rigid and is supported by the left. Practise at any reasonable distance from 10 yards upwards.

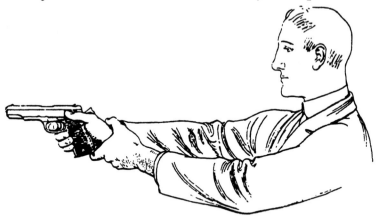

FIG. 15A.—Two-Handed, Standing.

Fig. 15 shows the proper method to employ if you have to shoot from the prone position (Fig. 16). Incidentally, do not be afraid to adopt this position immediately if circumstances demand it, as might be the case if you had to deal with several adversaries simultaneously. Practise yourself in getting quickly into the prone position, remembering that it gives you the dual advantage of being able to do your shooting from a steady position at a mark which is against the sky-line, as it were, while you yourself

FIG. 16.—Two-Handed, Prone.

offer a less conspicuous target for your opponents than if you were standing up.

Kind providence has endowed us all with a lively sense of self-preservation and some of us with a sense of strategy as well. If our readers are in the latter class we need not remind them of the advantages of taking cover whenever possible. It is possible, however, that some of you have not thought of a telephone pole or electric light standard in that connection. Fig. 17 will show you a side view of how to do it most conveniently, and Fig. 18 shows how an adversary will view the matter. Note in the former illustration the position of the feet, knees and left forearm. The left knee and forearm are pressed against the pole, left hand is grasping the right wrist, thumb of

D

Fig. 17.—Side View.

the right hand resting against
the pole. Fig. 18 also demon-
strates the almost perfect cover
provided.

If the long shot gives you
enough time to be deliberate,
so much the better, because the
two-handed position and that
of Fig. 17 permit of almost rifle-
like accuracy. But do not take
it for granted that you will
have time to be deliberate. It
is wiser to assume that you will
not, and it will be to your
advantage, therefore, to practise
all three of the two-handed
methods at the same surprise
targets as are used for short-
range work.

We have condemned the use
of sights for all forms of short-
range shooting, but for long
shots, such as we have been
describing, sights offer a distinct
advantage. We have little faith,
however, in those usually furnished. Good as some of them
are for use against a white
target and a black bull's eye,
there are very few that can

FIG. 18.—Front View.

be picked up instantly against a dark background, and this difficulty is increased to the point of being insuperable if the light is bad. To overcome this, the authors' personal pistols are fitted with foresights of silver, of exactly the shape of the ordinary shot-gun bead and about the same size. If kept bright, these sights collect any light there is from any angle and can be seen instantly in all circumstances except pitch-darkness. They stand up very well to rough work and can be easily replaced if damaged. We see no reason against the adoption of this type for service issue if some suitable white-metal alloy were used instead of silver. Though not claimed as suitable for target work, these sights answer their purpose admirably where speed is the prime consideration.

The best rear-sight for use in conjunction with the silver bead is a wide and shallow " V." The rear-sight should be affixed with a distinct slope to the rear, and once the gun is sighted-in, should be kept in place with a small set-screw. It will not shoot loose then and will be less liable to displacement or loss by accident or ill-usage.

CHAPTER V

PISTOL AND CARTRIDGE

Mechanical defects. Cartridge defects. Care
of ammunition. Supplies, current requirements and reserve stocks of ammunition.

THIS chapter relates only to the products of
manufacturing concerns of good standing and with
well-deserved reputations which they are not likely
to hazard. There are plenty of the other kind of
manufacturer but with them we have nothing to do
beyond remarking that it is due to their existence
that many criminals have been brought to justice
and the lives of many policemen have been saved.

The modern one-hand gun and its ammunition
have been brought to such a state of perfection that,
assuming reasonable care in their use, malfunctions
of the former and defects in the latter are of rare
occurrence.

The great majority of malfunctions of the modern
pistol are due, not to faults in design or manufacture,
but to ignorance, neglect or rough handling, accidental
or otherwise, on the part of the user.

Generally speaking, the private individual owning
a good pistol is too much of a " gun-crank " to be
guilty of wilful neglect or rough handling and to
him it is superfluous to recommend that, in case of

accident, his pistol should be promptly overhauled
by a competent armourer.

In the Services, however, matters are rather
different. Of necessity, very often, weapons are
subjected to rough treatment, and it may happen
that the most careful man may drop his pistol by
accident. If it is made clear to the men that such
accidents are not regarded as punishable offences,
they will be far more apt to report them quickly
and so ensure that their weapons, on which their
lives may depend, are put as soon as possible into
serviceable condition once more. We are not legis-
lating for the man who commits wilful damage or
the genius in whose hands everything comes to
pieces quite naturally. Men of that kind do not,
or should not, go very far without being recognised
for what they are, and there are suitable and well-
established methods of dealing with them.

As far as our experience goes, a comparison between
the automatic and the double-action revolver, in
respect of their liability to damage, results in favour
of the former.

Accident and ill-usage can have deplorable effects
on revolvers in the way of broken firing pins, damaged
pawls or cylinder ratchets and bent cranes, the last
mentioned giving rise to much more trouble than is
commonly supposed. Dropping the gun on to a
hard surface is often sufficient to put the crane out
of alignment, even though there is no visible damage
done, and no overhaul of a revolver is complete

unless the alignment of the crane is verified by the application of the requisite armourer's gauge. Then, too, there is the fact that barrel catch-springs, if of the flat or leaf variety, break far more frequently than they should, and it is surprising that manufacturers continue to fit them when it is a perfectly simple matter to substitute coil springs, which would be much more reliable.

An automatic of good make is much less liable than a revolver to damage from being dropped on a hard surface. The few instances of cracked slides are due, not to the weapon being dropped, but to long use in rapid fire, such as might be the case with a pistol used by an instructor. Nevertheless, a fall may damage the hammer and sights or may loosen pins and screws.

The extractors and ejectors occasionally give trouble, but this is usually due to wear after very long use.

Otherwise, there is little about the pistol itself that is liable to damage. We must look, rather, to its magazine for the cause of 90 per cent. of the troubles which we used to encounter, and in this connection we shall relate our own experiences in the care and maintenance of large numbers of automatic pistols having magazines of the detachable type.

We have to admit that in the beginning we paid little attention to the magazines or their condition. We soon noticed, however, that some of the magazines

in our charge were getting rusty and that others,
if not rusty, were clogged up with tobacco dust,
fluff and bits of matches, the sort of stuff that is
found in most men's pockets. We took the hint
and, as opportunity served, had every one of some
9000 magazines stripped and cleaned. The rust
was removed, together with astonishing quantities
of the stuff referred to above, and, more important
still, the overhaul served to reveal a certain amount
of damage due to hard knocks and wear and tear.
The only sensible thing to do was to recognise at
once the wear and tear that existed, and would
continue to exist, in an arduous service, the conditions
of which could not be modified, and then to apply
the remedy of periodic overhauls. It has long been
our custom, therefore, to have every pistol, with its
two magazines, sent to the armoury for inspection
at intervals of six months, regardless of whether or
not any defects are apparent. On these occasions,
not only do the pistols receive whatever attention
is necessary, but, as part of the routine, the magazines
are stripped and cleaned (reblued if they need it),
the springs are greased and, if found necessary, dents
are removed from the shells, base plates are
straightened out and splayed sides replaced in
position, the completed job having to measure up
to gauges specially constructed for each essential
dimension. The results of these periodic overhauls
have been entirely satisfactory and jambs are now
of rare occurrence.

Enough has been said to show that the condition of the magazine is of the utmost importance to the reliable functioning of the pistol and at least ordinary care, therefore, should be exercised in its regard. Those individuals who use their magazines as screwdrivers, or to open beer bottles, have no one to blame but themselves when their pistols refuse to function. If any doubt exists as to its condition, a magazine should be regarded as defective until competent inspection is available. If the doubt is confirmed, competent inspection will include a rapid-fire test with the magazine charged to full capacity. · A worthwhile precaution, to keep the spring efficient, is to remove one or two cartridges whenever circumstances permit. This applies, of course, to conditions which necessitate the magazine being kept charged more or less permanently. Properly treated, there is no reason why a well-made magazine should not last twenty years.

No ammunition can be expected to withstand indefinitely the wear and tear of daily use, which implies not only carrying it in all weathers but the frequent loading and unloading of weapons. It becomes necessary, therefore, first to ascertain the period for which ammunition may safely remain in daily use and then to withdraw it from circulation immediately the limit of that period has been reached.

Our conclusions in the matter are based upon the

exigencies of the police service of a great city, a
service that functions ceaselessly for twenty-four
hours a day and is maintained by large numbers
of men whom circumstances compel to go armed
with pistols. For a portion of the force, economy
demands a ratio of approximately two weapons to
three men. It is plain that the same men cannot be
on duty all the time and it follows that in the course
of twenty-four hours weapons and ammunition must
be returned at intervals to police stations for subsequent issue to other men going out on duty. Such
" change-overs," as they are known technically,
occur not less than three times in twenty-four hours.
At each " change-over " safety demands that the
weapons be unloaded, only to be reloaded on issue
to the next men. Apart from the " change-overs,"
which are due to motives of economy, it will be
recognised, too, that even in those cases where
weapons are provided for each individual, a certain
amount of loading and unloading is likely to take
place in the interests of safety. Add now the fact,
mentioned already, that the ammunition is carried
in all weathers and we have a set of circumstances
definitely indicative of hard usage.

Careful records of over fifteen years show that
under these circumstances the extreme length of
time for which automatic pistol ammunition can be
expected to be reliable is four months. Subsequently,
defects begin to be apparent and work out very
steadily at about two rounds per ten thousand. But

for every week thereafter the number of defective rounds increases with surprising rapidity. The records referred to show that revolver ammunition does not measure up to this standard. In point of fact, the ratio of defects is approximately double that of automatic pistol ammunition. The reasons are not far to seek.

The loading and unloading of revolvers imply much more handling of the ammunition than is the case with automatic pistols, which carry their ammunition in box magazines. Here the magazines receive most of the rough treatment. With all the care in the world we must expect, too, that occasionally ammunition will be dropped on the ground, possibly on the unsympathetic cement floor of a police station. Such treatment has less effect on automatic pistol ammunition, with its tightly crimped jacketed bullets, than on revolver cartridges, particularly those of large calibre carrying soft lead bullets. While there may be no noticeable deformation of the latter, they are more liable to be jarred loose from the crimping and that is the prelude to other troubles.

Apart from what may be regarded as inherent disadvantages in revolver ammunition, careful comparisons of respective measurements incline us to the belief that very often somewhat less care is exercised in its manufacture than is the case with automatic pistol ammunition. Of sheer necessity, the latter must conform more rigidly to accepted standards. Too great a departure from standard would be revealed very quickly by the automatic action of the weapon in which it is used, a compelling factor in the production of reliable ammunition. It is only fair to add that defects in the automatic ammunition put out by makers of repute are few and far between.

The " life " of ammunition is a matter which merits the most careful attention, particularly when we have to consider the needs of a service which is obliged to have a large amount in constant use. In some cases, too, complications arise from climatic conditions and distance from source of supplies.

It is possible to keep ammunition in excellent condition for a number of years provided that it is not removed from its cartons and packing-cases and that common-sense is used in the matter of storage. Having in mind the needs touched upon in the preceding paragraph, we prefer, however, not to trust to reserve supplies kept in stock for a number of years but to adopt instead what may be described as a " revolving credit." The tables given in the Appendix will convey our meaning more clearly, but we may state here that two basic conditions influence their construction, viz. :—

The undesirability of carrying ammunition in daily use for more than four months.
The undesirability of keeping ammunition in stock longer than two years.

From this as a starting point, quantities required on all counts can be estimated.

By means of this "revolving credit" system we are spared certain anxieties which would occur were reserve supplies to be kept in stock over a number of years. With our full supply expended in under two years, and replenished as necessary, we do not have to worry about such things as seasonal cracking or other forms of deterioration in the brass, deterioration of the smokeless powder charge, increased pressures due to that deterioration or, more important still, the reliability of the primers. We do not waste first-class ammunition on practice and training shoots, but use only that which we consider might be no longer reliable.

The reference to the reliability of the primers should be explained. We have in mind the modern non-fouling primer. It will be unnecessary for us to refer to its value in all circumstances, and particularly those in which the cleaning of weapons after firing has to be deferred longer than it should be. Up to date, however, it does not appear to last as long in adverse climatic conditions as the old rust-producing type. We admit that we are not quite sure of this, but while there is any doubt in the matter we prefer to take no more risks than we need, and this aspect is fully taken care of by the "revolving credit."

We think it will be helpful if our system of dealing

with the ammunition supply is closely linked with the armoury records which should be kept in respect of both ammunition and weapons.

Practice and training courses are invaluable in bringing to light any defective ammunition or pistols, which should be immediately withdrawn and sent to the armoury for examination.

If the examination reveals ammunition defects which are not due to ill-usage but to obvious faults in manufacture, the matter should be taken up with the makers, full records being kept. As regards the pistols, there should be a history sheet for each weapon and on it should be noted the attributed and actual causes of the defects (sometimes these differ widely), the repairs effected, the date returned to service and other appropriate data.

It is true that all this involves a certain amount of clerical work, but it is more than justified by the general efficiency which results and it sinks into insignificance when it is remembered what that efficiency may mean to men whose lives would otherwise be needlessly endangered.

CHAPTER VI

PRACTICAL PISTOL RANGES

DOUBTLESS most of us would prefer to do our pistol shooting out of doors. There is the pleasure of being in the fresh air, there are no powder fumes to contend with, and the noise is less trying than in an indoor range, where so many men find it necessary to plug their ears.

Apart, however, from these considerations, the value of an outdoor range is limited. It can only be used in daylight and in good weather. Further, though it may be a minor point, the equipment of an outdoor range is liable to deteriorate more rapidly than it would indoors. Influenced by the necessity to conduct pistol training regardless of weather and frequently after dark, our preference is for the indoor range. It gives us in addition greater facilities than would be reasonably possible out of doors for varying the lighting at will. We have in mind training courses which endeavour to reproduce as closely as possible the conditions which police the world over so often encounter in the course of duty. Criminals favour darkness or semi-darkness for the exercise of their talents, and a large proportion of the shooting affrays in which police are concerned take place under precisely those conditions. We venture to suggest that every man who has to use a pistol in the course of duty should learn how to do so in the dark. It *can* be done, it is often necessary, and the acquisition of confidence in this respect is invaluable.

If circumstances dictate an outdoor range, select, if you can, a piece of ground on which a high bank or a hillside provides a natural stop butt. A disused quarry or gravel-pit usually answers the purpose admirably. If the only ground available is flat, the stop butt is best constructed of a steeply sloping bank of earth backed by a wall of brick, stone, concrete or heavy timber.

Reference to the plan (Fig. 19) of an indoor range will show the lay-out we suggest. The contents of the next paragraph apply equally to outdoor and indoor ranges.

Every precaution must be taken against ricochets. The earth of which the stop butt is built up must be thoroughly sifted to ensure the removal of all stones, large and small. It is a good plan to face the sloping front of the stop butt with turf. Every scrap of metal used in the construction and which is liable to

---

* Fig. 19.

Explanation—

1, 1, 1. Frames for three bobbing targets, full figure.
2. Track and frame for running target, half figure.
3. Track and frame for running target, full figure.
4. Track and frame for running target, full figure.
5, 5, 5, 5, 5. Frames for five bobbing targets, half-figure.
6, 6, 6, 6. Frames for four disappearing targets, head and shoulder.

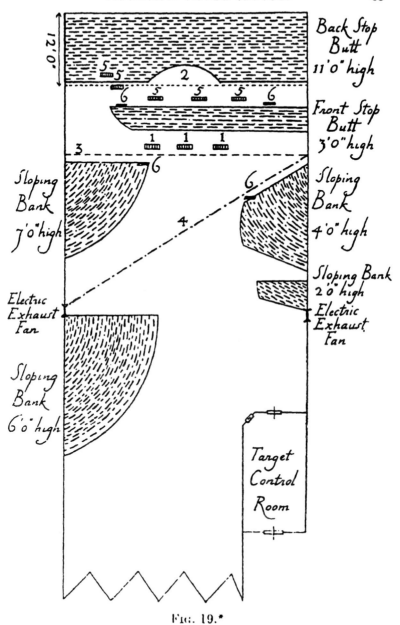

Fig. 19.*

be struck by bullets from the firing point must be
thoroughly protected by earth or soft wood. At
intervals, depending on the amount of shooting, the
stop butt should be raked and dug over in order to
remove all expended bullets. These do not penetrate
very far in any case, and continued firing con-
centrated on particular spots tends to bring them
to the surface. Their removal should not be deferred
too long, for being close to the surface of the bank
and most likely in agglomerations of many bullets
together, they constitute a definite cause of ricochets.
And no one can ever foretell the course (or force) of
a ricochet. The sale of the metal recovered in this
manner often helps materially to reduce the running
costs of a range. Prudence suggests that both the site
and the plans of construction should be approved
by the competent local authority before any work
is undertaken, and doubtless that authority will
insist on an examination of the completed range
before firing is permitted.

Reverting to the plan, we draw attention to one
feature that may be unusual and to another that
certainly is. The former is the Control Room, and
the latter is the absence of any fixed firing point.

The control room houses the men who operate
the targets. It provides them with perfect safety
while firing is in progress, and from it they emerge
at intervals to patch the targets. But they do not
emerge until the Range Officer switches on a green
light which shows high over the targets and is visible

to them. A red light is shown in the same place while firing is actually in progress or about to take place.

As stated, there is no fixed firing point nor is there any barrier across the range. The range is not divided into longitudinal sections, with booths for individual shooters at the firing end. Such devices would be impracticable for the training system which we advocate, and this will be clear if we add that we have to make provision for such widely differing demands as two-handed shooting at 25 yards, hip shooting at practically point-blank range; and practices which entail running at full speed a certain distance down the range in order to fire at several suddenly appearing moving targets. Obviously there is only room for one man at a time to shoot in safety under such conditions. The only time when this rule is permitted to be broken is in the initial recruit practices at stationary targets, when three men may sometimes shoot side by side, under the watchful eye of the instructor. It might be inferred from the fact that, with the one exception mentioned, only one man at a time can shoot, the proceedings would be unduly slow. In actual practice, however, the range illustrated and the system described have shown their capacity for a number of years to take care of the training and practice requirements of a force of 6000 men, or, if we include auxiliaries who also have to be trained, nearly 9000 men.

Freeing the range from all the obstacles that would

be constituted by fixed firing points also permits the
staging on occasion of what we are pleased to call
"mystery shoots." On these occasions the range,
except for the targets, is transformed beyond all
recognition, and it is astonishing what can be done
in this respect in a building of very modest dimensions.
To give an idea of what we mean, the range illustrated
on p. 65 has more than once been made to represent
the interior of a Chinese lodging-house harbouring,
among other inmates, half a dozen bad characters
who will resist arrest.

A screen hides all this from the men who are going
to shoot. All they see from the outside is a wall
with a door, through which, one by one, they will
have to enter the lodging-house. No one knows
what he will encounter inside, and the only
instructions given are that innocent civilians are not
to be "killed," such action being likely to impede
promotion. The first man to shoot pushes in the
door, closely followed by the range officer, and proceeds
with caution or with reckless abandon, according to
his nature, along a dark, narrow, twisting passage,
kicks open a door at one point, descends a few
steps, treads on floor-boards which give way under
him, climbs some more steps and finds himself in a
dimly lit room occupied by apparently harmless
people (dummies) who vary from mere lodgers to
dope fiends or stool-pigeons. He has to take in the
situation in a flash, for his appearance is the signal
for the fun to commence. A shot is fired at him

(blank cartridge in the control room), and the criminals commence their " get-away " (" criminals " are life-size targets that bob up from nowhere and disappear as quickly, heads and shoulders that peer at him briefly round a corner, men running swiftly across the room, possibly at an oblique angle, etc., all masked at some point in their careers by the " innocent bystanders," who must not be shot). There is no time to think, and anything resembling deliberate aim is a sheer impossibility. Furniture and dummies impede his movements, and it is noticeable that he instinctively adopts the " crouch " and shoots as a rule with the arm in any position except fully extended. His only course is to shoot quickly and keep on shooting till his magazine is empty, hoping that he is hitting the " criminals " and not the dummies. Any ill-luck as regards the latter is rewarded, when the results are announced, by precisely the sort of comment that might be expected from the crowd.

This sort of thing is not mere play-acting. It is done with the sole purpose of making practice as realistic as possible and of stimulating interest. If the men are kept indefinitely at the same dull routine they *will* lose interest, and results suffer accordingly.

We should add now that the expenses of these productions are negligible if there are available a little imagination, a lot of willing help, some wood battens, straw, old clothes and hessian or old sacking. The steps referred to are easily arranged by having a pit in the floor, keeping it covered over when not required. The loose flooring only requires a very simple bit of mechanism, worked from the control room, to make it give way slightly when walked on.

Targets, always life-size, are drawn or printed on the cheapest paper and pasted on to a backing of hessian, old cloth or canvas ; anything will do. This backing is tacked on to frames which are slid into trolleys, or hung on wires which are designed to provide the runners, bobbers, charging men, etc. to which reference has been made. These devices are all very simple and only need a little ingenuity to work out for any requirements. The target frames do not merit anything but the cheapest wood and roughest workmanship since they very quickly get shot to pieces.

Special attention must be given to the ventilation of the range, and there cannot well be too many exhaust-fans to carry away the powder fumes. Continued exposure to powder fumes is liable to produce an affection of the eyes which is in all respects similar to and indeed difficult to distinguish from conjunctivitis (" pink-eye "). The persons most liable to suffer from this complaint are the control room operators who spend much of their time in patching targets, and that is just where the fumes collect most thickly when firing at the very short distances which we advocate. The first signs of any inflammation of the eyes should be the signal to re-examine the ventilating system of the range.

We have found that the most practical flooring for the range is beaten earth. We think, too, that an earthen floor helps to reduce noise, which of course is considerably more in an indoor than an outdoor range. Noise can be reduced further by the use of millboard on the sides of the building and by curtains suspended from the roof or ceiling. The matter is largely one of experiment, and experiments in this direction are likely to be well worth the trouble involved.

CHAPTER VII

STOPPING POWER

WE approach this subject with considerable diffidence. We regard it as essentially one in which theory should be discarded in favour of practice, but even practice, as evidenced in carefully noted records over a number of years, does not lead us to any finality in the matter. Instead, it provides us with so many contradictions that we feel that anything approaching dogmatism would be most unwise.

To clear the ground for discussion we can eliminate at once the ·22's and ·25's, leaving only the larger calibres available in modern revolvers and automatic pistols. Those will be calibres ·32, ·38 and ·45, or approximately those sizes.

We were brought up in the belief that a heavy bullet of soft lead, travelling in the leisurely manner of bygone days, could not be improved upon if it was desired to dispose of one's human foes in a decisive and clean-cut manner. We believed that such a bullet would mushroom, and that even if it did not do so, the impact of such a formidable mass of lead would infallibly do all that was required, including knocking the enemy clean off his feet.

We also believed that bullets of approximately equal weight, jacketed with cupro-nickel and travelling at perhaps a greater velocity, provided penetration as opposed to shock and were therefore unsuited to their purpose ; and we had no faith whatever in light bullets driven at a much higher velocity, unless they could be so made as to secure effective expansion shortly after impact. Expanding bullets, however, are barred by the rules of the game as we have had to play it, so for practical purposes we must confine ourselves to solid bullets.

We are not so sure now of these beliefs. Perhaps the reasons for our doubts will be more easily apparent if we recount some actual experiences from the long list in our records. We shall make every effort to be impartial, and can assure our readers that in each case all data bearing on the subject was carefully sifted at the time and nothing has been preserved but actual facts.

We shall choose for our first instance one relating to the big lead bullet driven at a moderate velocity. On this occasion, a Sikh constable fired six shots with his ·455 Webley at an armed criminal of whom he was in pursuit, registering five hits. The criminal continued to run, and so did the Sikh, the latter clinching the matter finally by battering in the back of the criminal's head with the butt of his revolver. Subsequent investigations showed that one bullet only, and that barely deformed, remained in the body, the other four having passed clean through.

A very similar incident took place more recently —though it relates to a different weapon. A

European patrol-sergeant, hearing shooting and shouts of " Ch'iang-Tao " (robber), rushed to a rice shop which seemed to be the centre of the tumult, and there saw an armed Chinese robbing the till. The Chinese immediately opened fire on the sergeant with an automatic pistol at about 6 yards, firing several shots until his pistol jammed. Fortunately none of the shots took effect, and meanwhile the sergeant returned the fire swiftly and effectively with a ·45 Colt automatic, commencing at about 10 feet and firing his sixth and last shot at 3 feet as he rapidly closed in on his opponent. Later, it was found that of those six shots, four had struck fleshy parts of the body, passing clean through, while one bullet remained in the shoulder and another had lodged near the heart. Yet, in spite of all this, the robber was still on his feet and was knocked unconscious by the butt of the sergeant's pistol as he was attempting to escape by climbing over the counter. Here we have two heavy jacketed bullets which did not waste their substance on mere penetration, one of them inflicting a wound which came near to being fatal. In theory these two heavy bullets should have stopped the man in his tracks, but the facts are as related. Can anyone explain ?

Descending in the scale of calibres and bullet weights, the only record we have of a man dropping instantly when shot relates to the performance of a ·380 Colt automatic (pocket model). In this instance a single bullet penetrated from front to back, lodging very near the spine. The victim nevertheless recovered himself quickly and was able to get on his feet again. We think this case is probably analogous to the numerous instances that big-game hunters will recall of animals dropping instantly to neck shots that just miss the vertebra, only to get up again a few moments after and disappear over the horizon.

Turning now to the high velocity small calibre weapons, we have seen terrible damage caused by a Mauser automatic, calibre 7·63 mm., of military pattern. We have in mind the case of a man who was hit in the arm by a solid full-jacketed bullet from a weapon of this type. Though he was in hospital within half an hour of being shot, nothing could be done to avoid amputation, so badly were the bone and tissue lacerated. Perhaps " pulped " would convey our meaning more exactly. Yet in theory at least the bullet should have caused far less shock than it obviously did. From what we have read, the bullet had something of the effect that the latest developments in ultra high velocity small-bore rifles are reported to have on game animals. We might add that in the particular service from whose records we have been quoting, nothing is so feared, rightly or wrongly, as the Mauser military automatic. The mention of the word is sufficient, if there is trouble afoot, to send men in instant search of bullet-proof equipment.

We have tried to solve by experiment this question

of the knock-down blow, but there is no satisfactory
way of doing it. The nearest we have come to it
has been to allow ourselves to be shot at while
holding a bullet-proof shield. The chief value of
that experiment was a conclusive demonstration of
the efficacy of the shield.

Nevertheless, it did enable us to form some idea
of the disconcerting effect of the explosion when a
pistol is fired at one at very short range. These
experiments with bullet-proof shields amount to no
more than the firing of various types of bullets at a
very hard surface of considerable area, flexibly
supported, i.e. by the arm. The shock of impact
increased in proportion to the velocity of the bullets
but in all cases was negligible, the supporting arm
only recoiling minutely. The results to the bullets
were exactly what might have been expected. Soft
lead bullets at low velocity mushroomed perfectly,
jacketed bullets at moderate velocity broke into
sizable and greatly deformed fragments, while high
velocity jacketed bullets practically disintegrated.
But if the firing had been against a human body
instead of a shield, it would not be wise to conclude
either that the shock of impact would have been
so slight or that the various bullets would have
behaved exactly as they did.

Other tests, carried out by firing into wood of
varied thickness and hardness, very rarely showed
any appreciable deformation of bullets, even if they
were of soft lead.

These little experiments left us, however, with a query which we have not been able to answer. How much, if anything, of deformation or disintegration is due to the sudden arrestation of the rotary motion when bullets are fired from a rifled barrel at objects hard enough to resist them effectively ?

To sum up, all that we have done in this chapter is to provide instances of how various types of weapons and their loads have not run true to form. Preconceived ideas, based on theory or perhaps hearsay, seem to have been upset. We say " seem " advisedly, for in spite of the length and variety of our records we do not consider that we have had, even yet, sufficient visual proof of the behaviour and effects of bullets fired into human targets to enable us to lay down any hard-and-fast rules.

We do not know that a big soft lead bullet will not have the knock-down effect generally claimed. All we can say is that we have never seen it. We do not know for certain, either, that a full-jacketed high-velocity small-calibre bullet will always have the effect described in the particular instance which we have given.

We incline to the belief that the human factor must influence to some extent the behaviour of bullets. A pugilist at the top of his form can stand vastly more punishment than a man who is " soft " and untrained. Capacity to resist shock and pain appears to be also a function of the nervous system, and marked differences occur in this respect as between

individuals of different races. Perhaps that partially
explains why some men are not knocked out by bullets
when they ought to be. Again, if a bullet caught a
man off balance, might not that aid in producing the
appearance of a knock-down blow ?

We have made no mention yet of an aspect of this
matter which we have observed time after time in
the course of years. A hit in the abdominal region
almost invariably causes a man to drop anything he
may have in his hands and to clutch his stomach
convulsively. We may add that such a hit almost
always has fatal results, and that is an excellent
reason for such equipment as effective bullet-proof
vests, at least for the use of police.

If the ideal to be attained is a weapon that, with a
body shot alone, will drop a man in his tracks with
absolute certainty, then there is something lacking
in the best of modern revolvers and automatics. It
could be done, doubtless, with a weapon of greatly
increased calibre and power, but the added weight
and size of such a weapon would almost certainly
render it unsuitable for average requirements. So
perhaps we shall have to make the best of such
weapons as are available to us.

Those readers who have had the patience to follow
us so far will most likely be justifiably irritated by
our inconclusiveness. We can imagine them saying,
" But there must be one or two kinds of pistol that
are better than all the others. Why on earth can't
they tell us what they are ? "

If that question is asked, we should reply that, for ourselves, we should choose the pistol which, while being easy to carry and convenient to use, would conform most nearly with the following requirements :—

(1) The maximum of stopping power.
(2) The maximum volume of fire.
(3) The maximum speed of discharge.

To attain the first requirement we should choose a cartridge that represents what we consider a safe middle course, *i.e.* with a bullet of reasonably large calibre and weight, driven at a very high velocity.

As regards the second requirement the reader will have gathered from Chapters III and IV on training that we have a preference for firing in " bursts " of two or more shots. We think that lack of stopping power inherent in the cartridge is compensated for in some degree by the added shock of two or more shots in very rapid succession. Medical evidence tends to confirm this belief, which is strengthened moreover by the evidences we have seen of the terribly destructive effects on human targets of submachine-guns of the Thompson type. Obviously, this belief of ours implies the necessity for a large volume of fire, quite apart from the desirability on other grounds of having as many rounds as possible at one's disposal without having to reload.

Throughout this book we have done our best to

emphasise the vital need for extreme rapidity of fire. For ourselves we can accomplish this, our third desideratum, most easily with an automatic. The more closely our own pistols resemble machine-guns the better we like it.

CHAPTER VIII

MISCELLANEOUS

Holsters. Care and Cleaning of Pistols.

HOLSTERS for service men who are required to carry a pistol openly while in uniform must obviously be of a standard pattern, and there is little room for all the refinements that go to the making of a really good holster where individual requirements are the only consideration.

Nevertheless, the design of service holsters might well be given a little more thought than is often the case. It is not possible, perhaps, to combine service needs with the facilities for the lightning-quick draw which some special designs provide, but there are one or two things that can be done to help in the latter respect. The butt of the pistol should protrude from the holster sufficiently to allow the user to get it well into his hand as quickly as possible; there should be no fumbling. If there is, there is something radically wrong with the design. The front of the holster should be cut away to allow the forefinger to enter the trigger-guard without resistance and without the stubbing of the finger-nail on the leather that is so often noticed. The gun can be secured in the holster either by a flap or a strap, both fastening on a metal stud. The strap is, of course, no wider

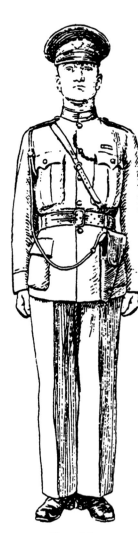

FIG. 20.

than it must be to effect its purpose. The flap offers better protection from the weather, and we do not think its greater width makes any real difference to the speed with which the pistol can be drawn. The bottom of the holster should be open so that in case of rain or accidental immersion the water does not remain inside and the holster can dry out more quickly: The bottom of the holster cannot be entirely open if the design of the pistol is such that it will slip too far down, but it is always possible to leave an aperture or apertures of adequate size for draining.

There remains to be considered the position in which the holster should be worn. The writers have a preference for wearing the gun on the belt at the left side of the body. In that position (see Fig. 20) the wearer is able to draw his pistol at reasonable speed, and apart from those occasions when he is obliged to shoot, he can protect it with his left hand and forearm from attempts to snatch it from the holster. Policemen find that such attempts are by no means infrequent in a crowd or on the part of " drunks " resisting arrest. To guard further against this danger (and it may well be serious), we recommend the use of a stout lanyard attached at one end to the swivel in the pistol butt. The other end should pass in a loop over the right shoulder, the shoulder strap of the uniform preventing the lanyard from slipping off. Never wear the lanyard round the neck, as we have sometimes seen it done, for needless to say, such a practice is liable to add to the danger very considerably.

Whatever the position in which the holster is worn, great care should be taken to ensure that its design and method of attachment to the belt provide the maximum of resistance when the pistol is drawn. To make our meaning clearer, the pistol should slip easily out of the holster, but the holster itself should remain as nearly immovable as possible. Otherwise, when the pistol is drawn, the holster has a tendency to accompany it, and the result is a slow and clumsy draw. With a holster worn on the right thigh, the necessary amount of resistance may have to be provided by a thong or string fastened to the bottom of the holster and tied round the leg. Though so far we have been referring solely to holsters to be worn openly when in uniform, it will be obvious that the necessity for resistance exists for all other holsters as well.

Turning now to holsters for other purposes, we strongly recommend the reader to be satisfied only with the best and to take any amount of trouble in order to get it.

Having provided yourself with the pistol of your choice, consider next how it will suit you best to carry it. Determine whether it is to be carried openly or concealed on the person. If the latter, do you prefer it under the left arm (Figs. 21 and 21A, pp. 85, 86) or around the waist (see Figs. 22, 22A, 22B, pp. 87, 88)? Having decided these points, get in touch with one of the reliable and well-known makers of holsters. If unable to visit him personally, provide him with such information as is appropriate to your requirements. Depending on those requirements, such information might well consist of

The make and model of the pistol.
Your chest, waist and shoulder measurements.
Length of arm.
Size of hand and length and thickness of trigger-finger.
A photograph of yourself, showing the clothes usually worn.

With these particulars in his possession, the maker will be able to design a holster suited to your requirements in every way, including the correct angle at which to wear it. This latter is a most

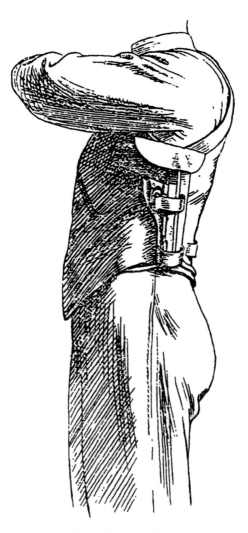

Fig. 21.—Shoulder Holster.

Fig. 21a.—Shoulder Holster.

FIG. 22.—Belt-Holster and Pistol.

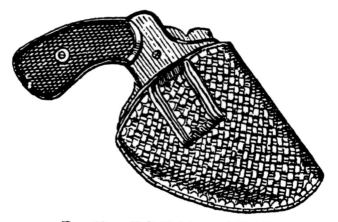

FIG. 22A.—Belt-Holster and Pistol.

FIG. 22B.—Cut-down Revolver.

important aid to a quick draw. Though the fore-going may appear to the uninitiated as unduly meticulous, if not altogether too "finicky," it is only in this way that you will be able to get the utmost out of the pistol of your choice. That, we presume, is your object, and that to attain it you will be prepared to go to the necessary trouble and expense.

Supposing now that you have obtained a good holster, do not put it away and forget it. Mere possession is not sufficient. The best holster ever made will not make you any quicker on the draw without practice, and plenty of it. Nothing can excel "dry" practice in front of a mirror, and a friend with a stop-watch can often help you materially.

Though it is a safe general rule to seek the assist-ance of a manufacturer of repute, we should be the first to admit that there are plenty of other ingenious people capable of thinking out, designing and even making extremely effective holsters for themselves. One of the fastest holsters we have ever seen was designed and made by an amateur for use when on motor-cycle patrol. Fashioned from a cut-down service holster and fastened on with pieces of string, the finished product was not a thing of beauty, but it was 100 per cent. practical. It hung slightly below his belt in the centre of his body and enabled him to drop his hand a few inches from the handle-bar of the cycle on to the butt of the gun with complete certainty and lightning speeed. Moreover, the holster held the gun securely even when riding

over very rough ground. Here is a case of a man
who not only had sufficient ingenuity to make a
holster which exactly met his particular requirements,
but sufficient application to perfect himself in its
use by assiduous " dry " practice.

Another instance of ingenuity on the part of an
amateur, though it relates more nearly to a " gadget "
than a holster, was furnished by a doctor whom one
of the authors met in San Diego. This device was
intended to cope with a " hold-up " when driving
his motor-car. A slight flick of his hands and the
next instant the doctor was grasping a pair of
·38 revolvers, all ready for instant action. The
observer's impression was that the guns appeared
from nowhere, and far too quickly to enable one to
get any idea how it was done. Had the doctor been
actually held up at the moment, it is more than likely
that his assailant would have been completely beaten
by the utter unexpectedness of the thing.

We should not attempt to describe the device
even if we could. It is sufficient to say that it was
the result of many weeks of planning, adjustment
and "dry" practice, all of which the doctor found
to be " well worth the trouble, and great fun besides."

On the same day, the author referred to was
privileged to watch the Martin Brothers at quick-draw
work with their famous front-draw holsters, one
strapped down on each thigh, and he left firmly
convinced that San Diego would be a very good
town for bad men to keep away from.

CARE OF PISTOLS AND METHOD OF CLEANING

In one respect the pistol resembles the automobile engine or other piece of machinery in that it should be " run-in " and subsequently " tuned-up " to remove any small defects and asperities. This applies with greater force to automatics, and in their case the " running-in " process may well consist of fifty rounds of rapid fire. If all bearing-parts are then smoothed up by an armourer who knows his business, the pistols will not only be pleasanter to shoot with but will last much longer.

Where a number of men are engaged in cleaning their pistols at the same time, care must be taken that all parts which have been dismounted are reassembled on the right pistols. To this end, it is of great advantage if such parts are all stamped plainly with the numbers borne by the respective pistols to which they belong. This also ensures that pistols are correctly reassembled by the armourers after a general overhaul.

Cleaning in these days is a simple matter. Provide yourself with a celluloid-covered cleaning rod, the tip threaded to receive any of the following implements—a brass wire brush, a slotted jag, and a bristle brush. Provide yourself also with an aqueous solvent (of the nature of " Chloroil " or Young's ·303 Cleaner), some flannelette patches and a tube of gun grease.

If the pistol permits of it, dismantle it, to facilitate

the cleaning of the barrel. Attach the brass wire brush to the rod, dip it into the solvent, and run it through the barrel several times to loosen the fouling, and more particularly, if your ammunition has the older type of primer, to remove the potassium chloride which in that case will have been deposited. Then, using the slotted jag, run through several patches soaked with the solvent, finishing with one or two dry patches. The last dry patch should bear no traces of fouling. Finish with an application of the gun grease on the bristle brush. There should be no more grease than is necessary to coat the inside of the barrel with a *very light film* and *neither breech nor muzzle should be choked or clogged up.* If care is exercised in these respects, the pistol may be fired subsequently without having to wipe the barrel out first.

Whenever the design of the pistol permits it, always clean the barrel from the breech end.

All the foregoing remarks apply to barrels of automatic pistols and barrels and cylinders of revolvers.

Incidentally, nickel fouling due to jacketed bullets does not appear to exist. If it does, it is so slight as to be of no account.

The major part of the task is now finished. For the rest, wipe over with a slightly greasy rag all other metal parts, paying particular attention to the breech face, and in the case of revolvers to the other parts where fouling is apt to collect.

If the pistol is to be put away for any length of time, wipe dry and clean all metal parts other than the barrel (which has been attended to already), apply a film of gun grease (most easily done with the bristle brush) and wrap in greaseproof paper, making sure that you do not leave finger-marks on the metal. A pistol treated in this manner and put away in its box or case, if you have one, may be stored for a long time without attention. Never store in a holster ; the leather is susceptible to damp and will cause rusting of all metal in contact with it.

We do not favour the use of oil. If it is too thin it is not a good preservative, and if it is too thick it is liable to become gummy, to the detriment of moving parts. Almost invariably, too, its use is overdone, with the result that the pistol overflows with oil which cannot all be removed before firing. Firing, and more particularly rapid firing, is apt to cause the user to be bespattered with this excess of oil. It is neither useful nor pleasant and is best avoided altogether. Lubrication of such moving parts as can be seen is just as well accomplished by use of the gun grease, applied sparingly with the bristle brush. The grease does not melt, dry off or spatter. Lubrication of locks, etc., should be a matter for the armourer. Locks do not need much lubrication in any case, and are only liable to be gummed up from the usual practise of squirting oil into the interior of the mechanism through every available aperture.

APPENDIX

AMMUNITION

" Revolving Credit " System, referred to on p. 60.

THE unit quantities given in Table I are approximately those which have been found to answer our own purposes, but can be varied, of course, to suit different needs or the requirements of larger or smaller numbers of men. For greater simplicity, Table I is assumed to provide for a force of 1000 men.

TABLE I
Requirements over Twelve Months

	Rounds
To be carried in daily use by each man, 12 rounds . . .	× 1000 = 12,000
Practice and training, 36 rounds per man	× 1000 = 36,000
In reserve, 30 rounds per man .	× 1000 = 30,000
	78,000

An initial purchase is made of the total· quantity indicated by Table I as required over a period of twelve months and, for added clarity, we shall assume that it is on hand at the end of December.

TABLE II
Disposal of Initial Purchase

1st January—   Rounds
Place to reserve 30,000
Issue for daily use 12,000
Issue for training and practice . . 12,000

1st May—
Withdraw 12,000 issued 1st January (for
daily issue) and use for training and
practice. Replace for daily use, by fresh
issue of 12,000

1st September—
Withdraw 12,000 issued 1st May (for daily
use) and use for training and practice.
Replace for daily use, by fresh issue of . 12,000

           78,000

In twelve months, therefore, 36,000 rounds have been actually expended in training and practice.

Meanwhile, a second but smaller purchase has been made and is on hand at the end of December, twelve months after the first purchase arrived, so that the stock of ammunition is as shown in the next table.

TABLE III
Stock at end of First Twelve Months   Rounds

In reserve 30,000
In daily use (issued 1st September) . . 12,000
Amount of second purchase 36,000

           78,000

We commence the second year with a stock of the same quantity as that with which we began originally and so are able to repeat exactly the processes of the first year.

There is one difference to be noted, however. The second purchase is not drawn on until the first is exhausted. Thus on 1st January of the second year, 12,000 rounds, issued for daily use at the beginning of the preceeding September, are withdrawn and issued for training and practice, their place being taken by 12,000 from reserve. The May issue, 12,000, and half the September issue, 6000, completely exhausted the 30,000 originally placed to reserve.

Our two basic conditions are therefore fulfilled, i.e. :

> No ammunition in daily use longer than four months.
>
> No ammunition in stock longer than two years.

As long as the programme is adhered to, the processes outlined are merely a matter of repetition year after year.